PRAYING GOD'S WILL *for* MY LIFE

LEE ROBERTS

THOMAS NELSON
Since 1798

Published in Nashville, Tennessee, by Oliver Nelson Books, a
division of Thomas Nelson, Inc.

The Bible version used in this publication is THE NEW KING
JAMES VERSION. Copyright © 1979, 1980, 1982. Thomas Nelson,
Inc., Publishers. Verses have been modified to fit the prayer format.

Library of Congress Cataloging-in-Publication Data

Roberts, Lee, 1941–
    Praying God's will for my life / Lee Roberts.
        p. cm.
    ISBN 10: 0-7852-6584-8 (pbk.)
    ISBN 13: 978-0-7852-6584-9
    1. Prayer—Christianity. 2. God—Will. 3. Christian life—1960–
I. Title.

BV215.R58 1993
242–dc20   93–4500
                                                            CIP

Printed in Mexico
06 07 08 09 QW 10 9 8 7 6

To the Lord Jesus Christ

ANGER

Heavenly Father, I thank You for all that You do for me. During this time of being alone with You, I ask You, in Jesus' name, to hear Your Word as my prayers concerning any anger that may abide in me. Your Word is clear that anger does not produce righteousness in me. I petition You now, with Your very words, to remove any anger from me that may be a stumbling block in my walk with You. Thank You, God. Amen.

GOD, IN ACCORDANCE WITH YOUR WORD . . .

I pray that I will let all bitterness, wrath, anger, clamor, and evil speaking be put away from me, along with all malice. I pray also that I will be kind to others, tenderhearted, forgiving others, just as You in Christ forgave me.

EPHESIANS 4:31–32

I pray that I will be swift to hear, slow to speak, slow to wrath; for my wrath does not produce Your righteousness.

JAMES 1:19–20

I pray that my discretion makes me slow to anger, and that it is to my glory to overlook a transgression.

PROVERBS 19:11

I pray that I will commit my way to You, LORD, and trust also in You, and that You shall bring it to pass. You shall bring forth my righteousness as the light, and my justice as the noonday. I pray that I will rest in You, LORD, and wait patiently for You; I pray that I do not fret because of him who prospers in his way, or because of the man who brings wicked schemes to pass. I pray that I will cease from anger, and forsake wrath; that I do not fret—it only causes harm.

PSALM 37:5–8

I pray that I will not hasten in my spirit to be angry, for anger rests in the bosom of fools.

ECCLESIASTES 7:9

⌒

I pray that I understand that a fool vents all his feelings, but a wise man holds them back.

PROVERBS 29:11

⌒

I pray that I know that being slow to anger is better than the mighty, and ruling my spirit is better than taking a city.

PROVERBS 16:32

⌒

I pray that I will make no friendship with an angry person, and with a furious person I do not go, lest I learn his ways and set a snare for my soul.

PROVERBS 22:24–25

I pray that when I am angry, I will not sin. I pray that I do not let the sun go down on my wrath.

EPHESIANS 4:26

I pray that I realize that a quick-tempered person acts foolishly.

PROVERBS 14:17

I pray that I always remember that a soft answer turns away wrath, but a harsh word stirs up anger.

PROVERBS 15:1

ATTITUDE

Lord Jesus, I ask You now, using the words that have been given to me in the Holy Scriptures, to make certain that I always have an attitude of joy in You. Give me an attitude and an expectancy that I can do all things through You who give me strength to face the issues and problems of life. Thank You, Lord, for my happiness and my joy. In Your name I pray. Amen.

GOD, IN ACCORDANCE WITH YOUR WORD . . .

I pray that I will remember whatever things are true, whatever things are noble, whatever things are just, whatever things are pure, whatever things are lovely, whatever things are of good report, if there is any virtue and if there is anything praiseworthy—I will meditate on these things.

PHILIPPIANS 4:8

3

CONDEMNED

Lord God, I come before You at this moment to ask You to keep in my mind at all times that there is no condemnation for those who are in Christ Jesus. Help me to know that if I trust in Jesus, I need not let Satan bring thoughts of doubt and condemnation to my mind. Thank You, Lord, for removing all such thoughts and feelings from me. In Jesus' name. Amen.

GOD, IN ACCORDANCE WITH YOUR WORD . . .

I pray that I will draw near with a true heart in full assurance of faith, having my heart sprinkled from an evil conscience and my body washed with pure water.

HEBREWS 10:22

I pray that I always remember that You, the LORD my God, are gracious and merciful, and will not turn Your face from me if I return to You.

2 CHRONICLES 30:9

I pray that I believe the truth of what You, God, said: "I, even I, am He who blots out your transgressions for My own sake."

ISAIAH 43:25

Thank You, God, that You did not send Your Son into the world to condemn me, but that I through Him might be saved. I who believe in Him am not condemned.

JOHN 3:17–18

I pray that I, who hear Your word, and believe in You, God, who sent Jesus, have everlasting life, and that I shall not come into judgment, but have passed from death into life.

JOHN 5:24

I pray that You, God, will be merciful to my unrighteousness, and to my sins and my lawless deeds, and that You will remember them no more.

HEBREWS 8:12

I pray that I will forsake any wicked ways and any unrighteous thoughts. Let me return to You, LORD, and You will have mercy on me and abundantly pardon me.

ISAIAH 55:7

I pray that as far as the east is from the west, so far have You removed my transgressions from me.

PSALM 103:12

I pray that if I am in You, Christ, I am a new creation; old things have passed away; behold, all things have become new.

2 CORINTHIANS 5:17

I pray that I will acknowledge my sin to You, God, and my iniquity I will not hide. I pray that I will confess my transgressions to You so You can forgive the iniquity of my sin.

PSALM 32:5

I pray that if I will confess my sins, You, God, are faithful and just to forgive my sins and to cleanse me from all unrighteousness.

1 JOHN 1:9

Thank You for promising that there is therefore now no condemnation to me because I am in Christ Jesus. I pray that I do not walk according to the flesh, but according to the Spirit. For the law of the Spirit of life in Christ Jesus has made me free from the law of sin and death.

ROMANS 8:1–2

I pray that I am blessed, that my transgression is forgiven, that my sin is covered.

PSALM 32:1

I pray that I have overcome Satan by the blood of the Lamb and by the word of my testimony.

REVELATION 12:11

I pray that I remember that Jesus said, "Neither do I condemn you; go and sin no more."

JOHN 8:11

I pray, God, that You will forgive my iniquity, and my sin You will remember no more.

JEREMIAH 31:34

4

CONFIDENCE

Lord Jesus, based on God's Word I call upon You to fill me with confidence. Give me the spiritual confidence to know that whatever I ask in Your name I will receive. Fill me with the confidence that only You can give. Thank You for honoring Your Word and my prayers. Amen.

GOD, IN ACCORDANCE WITH YOUR WORD . . .

I pray that when I pass through the waters, You will be with me; and through the rivers, they shall not overflow me. When I walk through the fire, I shall not be burned, nor shall the flame scorch me. For You are the LORD my God.

ISAIAH 43:2–3

I pray, God, that I always remember that it is You who justify.

ROMANS 8:33

I pray that this is the confidence that I have in You, Jesus, that if I ask anything according to Your will, You hear me. And if I know that You hear me, whatever I ask, I know that I have the petitions that I have asked of You.

1 JOHN 5:14–15

I pray that when I face an obstacle, I always remember that You said that it is "not by might nor by power, but by My Spirit."

ZECHARIAH 4:6

I pray that whatever I ask in Jesus' name, You will do it.

JOHN 14:14

I pray that You, the LORD God, are my strength.

HABAKKUK 3:19

I pray that I will not cast away my confidence, which has great reward. For I have need of endurance, so that after I have done the will of You, God, I may receive the promise.

HEBREWS 10:35–36

I pray that I will be confident of this very thing, that You who have begun a good work in me will complete it until the day of Jesus Christ.

PHILIPPIANS 1:6

I pray that I can do all things through Christ who strengthens me.

PHILIPPIANS 4:13

I pray that I may boldly say: "The LORD is my helper; I will not fear. What can man do to me?"

HEBREWS 13:6

I pray that if my heart does not condemn me, I will have confidence toward You, God.

1 JOHN 3:21

I pray that if I will wait on You, LORD, I shall renew my strength. I shall mount up with wings like eagles, I shall run and not be weary, I shall walk and not faint.

ISAIAH 40:31

5

CONFUSED

Heavenly Father, in the beautiful and precious name of Jesus, my Lord and Savior, I ask You to remove all confusion from me. Help me to know that You are the author of peace and not of confusion, and that I am to lean on You and Your Word and not my own understanding. Thank You in Jesus' name for honoring my prayer.

GOD, IN ACCORDANCE WITH YOUR WORD . . .

I pray that I will trust in You, LORD, with all my heart, and lean not on my own understanding. I pray that in all my ways I will acknowledge You, and You shall direct my paths.

PROVERBS 3:5–6

I pray that You, God, will instruct me and teach me in the way I should go.

PSALM 32:8

I pray that I have great peace because I love Your law, and nothing can cause me to stumble.

PSALM 119:165

I pray that I will always cast my burdens on You, LORD, and You shall sustain me.

PSALM 55:22

I pray that when I pass through the waters, You will be with me. And when I pass through the rivers, they shall not overflow me. When I walk through the fire, I shall not be burned, nor shall the flame scorch me. For You are the LORD my God.

ISAIAH 43:2–3

I pray that I will be anxious for nothing, but in everything by prayer and supplication, with thanksgiving, let my requests be made known to You, God; and Your peace, which surpasses all understanding, will guard my heart and mind through Christ Jesus.

PHILIPPIANS 4:6–7

I pray that I will always remember that You give power to the weak, and to those who have no might You increase strength.

ISAIAH 40:29

I pray that I know that where envy and self-seeking exist, confusion and every evil thing are there. But the wisdom that is from above is first pure, then peaceable, gentle, willing to yield, full of mercy and good fruits, without partiality and without hypocrisy.

JAMES 3:16—17

I pray that when I feel confused, I will remember and understand that You, God, are not the author of confusion but of peace.

1 CORINTHIANS 14:33

I pray, God, that I will remember that You have not given me a spirit of fear, but of power and of love and of a sound mind.

2 TIMOTHY 1:7

I pray that You, Lord GOD, will help me;
therefore I will not be disgraced.

ISAIAH 50:7

I pray that I will not think it strange concerning
the fiery trial which is to try me, as though some
strange thing happened to me; but that I will
rejoice to the extent that I partake of Christ's
sufferings, that when His glory is revealed, I may
also be glad with exceeding joy.

1 PETER 4:12–13

I pray that if I lack wisdom, I will ask of You,
God, who give to all liberally and without
reproach, and it will be given to me.

JAMES 1:5

6

COURAGE

Perfect God, grant me the courage that only
You can give. Help me to remember that You
promised in Your Word that I can do all things
through Jesus, and that I should never be afraid
or discouraged or dismayed because You, my
God, will be with me always. Thank You, God, in
Jesus' name, for filling me with courage. Amen.

GOD, IN ACCORDANCE WITH YOUR WORD . . .

I pray that I will always fear not, for You, God,
are with me. I pray that I will not be dismayed,
for You are my God. I pray that You will
strengthen me and help me, and that You will
uphold me with Your righteous right hand.

ISAIAH 41:10

I pray that I will be persuaded that neither death nor life, nor angels nor principalities nor powers, nor things present nor things to come, nor height nor depth, nor any other created thing, shall be able to separate me from the love of God which is in Christ Jesus my Lord.

ROMANS 8:38—39

I pray that I shall not die, but live, and declare the works of the LORD.

PSALM 118:17

I pray that You, the eternal God, are my refuge, and that You will thrust out the enemy from before me.

DEUTERONOMY 33:27

I pray that I can do all things through Christ who strengthens me.

PHILIPPIANS 4:13

I pray that I will wait on You, LORD; that I will be of good courage, and You shall strengthen my heart.

PSALM 27:14

I pray that I do not think it strange concerning the fiery trial which is to try me, as though some strange thing happened to me; but that I will rejoice to the extent that I partake of Christ's sufferings, that when His glory is revealed, I may also be glad with exceeding joy.

1 PETER 4:12–13

I pray that when I pass through the waters, You will be with me; and through the rivers, they shall not overflow me. When I walk through the fire, I shall not be burned, nor shall the flame scorch me. For You are the LORD my God.

ISAIAH 43:2–3

I pray that I will remember that while my
weeping may endure for a night, joy comes to
me in the morning.

PSALM 30:5

I pray that I will be of good courage, and You
shall strengthen my heart, for my hope is in You,
LORD.

PSALM 31:24

I pray that I will wait on You, LORD, and that I
shall renew my strength. I pray that I shall
mount up with wings like eagles; that I shall run
and not be weary, that I shall walk and not faint.

ISAIAH 40:31

I pray that I will be anxious for nothing, but in
everything by prayer and supplication, with
thanksgiving, will let my requests be made
known to You, God.

PHILIPPIANS 4:6

I pray that whatever things are true, whatever things are noble, whatever things are just, whatever things are pure, whatever things are lovely, whatever things are of good report, if there is any virtue and if there is anything praiseworthy—that I will meditate on these things.

PHILIPPIANS 4:8

I pray that I shall obtain joy and gladness, and that sorrow and sighing shall flee away.

ISAIAH 51:11

7

DELIVERANCE

Lord Jesus, today, at this very moment, I ask You to deliver me from anything that is adversely afflicting me in any way. Help me to know the truth that comes only from You and Your Word, and to be set free from all that is upon me. Thank You, Jesus, for freeing me and for filling me with joy and hope. Amen.

GOD, IN ACCORDANCE WITH YOUR WORD . . .

I pray that I shall know the truth, and the truth shall make me free.

JOHN 8:32

I pray that if You, Jesus, make me free, I shall be free indeed.

JOHN 8:36

I pray that I remember that there is therefore
now no condemnation to me who is in Christ
Jesus, and that I do not walk according to the
flesh, but according to the Spirit. For the law of
the Spirit of life in Christ Jesus has made me free
from the law of sin and death.

ROMANS 8:1–2

I pray that I do not believe every spirit, but that I
test the spirits, whether they are of You, God;
because many false prophets have gone out into
the world. I pray that by this I will know Your
Spirit: Every spirit that confesses that Jesus Christ
has come in the flesh is of You, God.

1 JOHN 4:1–2

I pray that I will always know that He who is in
me is greater than he who is in the world.

1 JOHN 4:4

I pray that I have overcome Satan by the blood of the Lamb and by the word of my testimony.

REVELATION 12:11

8

DEPRESSED

Lord God, I pray to You now, as always, in Jesus' name. I ask You to remove any depression that may come upon me at any time. Help me to know that if I will cry out to You that You will hear and deliver me. I ask You to honor Your Word and deliver me from any depression that I may ever experience. In Jesus' name. Amen.

GOD, IN ACCORDANCE WITH YOUR WORD . . .

I pray that I will cry out, and You will hear and deliver me out of all of my troubles.

PSALM 34:17

I pray, God, that You are the God of my strength.

PSALM 43:2

I pray that while my weeping may endure for a night, my joy comes in the morning.

PSALM 30:5

◡

I pray that I will wait on You, LORD. That I shall renew my strength. That I shall mount up with wings like eagles, I shall run and not be weary, and that I shall walk and not faint.

ISAIAH 40:31

◡

I pray, God, that You will comfort me in all my tribulation, that I may be able to comfort those who are in any trouble, with the comfort with which I myself am comforted by You.

2 CORINTHIANS 1:4

I pray that I am persuaded that neither death nor life, nor angels nor principalities nor powers, nor things present nor things to come, nor height nor depth, nor any other created thing, shall be able to separate me from Your love, God, which is in Christ Jesus my Lord.

ROMANS 8:38—39

I pray that I do not think it strange concerning the fiery trial which is to try me, as though some strange thing happened to me; but that I will rejoice to the extent that I partake of Christ's sufferings, so that when His glory is revealed, I may also be glad with exceeding joy.

1 PETER 4:12—13

I pray that whatever things are true, whatever things are noble, whatever things are just, whatever things are pure, whatever things are lovely, whatever things are of good report, if there is any virtue and if there is anything praiseworthy—that I will meditate on these things.

PHILIPPIANS 4:8

I pray, God, that You will heal my broken heart and bind up my wounds.

PSALM 147:3

I pray that I will fear not, for You are with me. That I will not be dismayed, for You are my God. I pray that You will strengthen me; that You will help me and that You will uphold me with Your righteous right hand.

ISAIAH 41:10

I pray that I will humble myself under Your mighty hand, God, that You may exalt me in due time. I pray that I will cast all my cares upon You, for You care for me.

1 PETER 5:6—7

I pray that I will always pray and not lose heart.

LUKE 18:1

I pray that I will not sorrow, for the joy of the LORD is my strength.

NEHEMIAH 8:10

9

DESERTED BY LOVED ONES

Heavenly Father, I plead with You at this moment to honor Your Word and set me on high. Your Word has promised that You will never leave me nor forsake me, no matter what my loved ones might do. I need You now. Draw me close to You and carry my burdens for me. In the name of Your Son, Jesus, I pray. Amen.

GOD, IN ACCORDANCE WITH YOUR WORD . . .

I pray that because You have set Your love upon me, You will deliver me. You will set me on high, because I have known Your name. I pray that I shall call upon You, and You will answer me. That You will be with me in trouble. That You will deliver me and honor me. That with long life You will satisfy me and show me Your salvation.

PSALM 91:14—16

I pray, God, that You will not forsake me nor
destroy me.

DEUTERONOMY 4:31

I pray that I will cast all my cares upon You, God,
for You care for me.

1 PETER 5:7

I pray that while I am hard-pressed on every side,
I am not crushed; I am perplexed, but not in
despair; persecuted, but not forsaken; struck
down, but not destroyed—always carrying about
in my body the dying of the Lord Jesus, that the
life of Jesus also may be manifested in my body.

2 CORINTHIANS 4:8–10

I pray that I shall no longer be forsaken, and You
will delight in me.

ISAIAH 62:4

I pray that because I know Your name, God, I will put my trust in You; for You, LORD, have not forsaken those who seek You.

PSALM 9:10

⌒

I pray that if my father and my mother forsake me, then You will take care of me.

PSALM 27:10

⌒

I pray that I will be taught to observe all things that Jesus has commanded, and that I know that You are with me always, even to the end of the age.

MATTHEW 28:20

⌒

I pray that I always remember that You will not forget me.

ISAIAH 49:15

I pray that my hope is in You, God, and that I shall yet praise You, the help of my countenance and my God.

PSALM 43:5

I pray that I will be strong and of good courage. That I will not fear nor be afraid; for You, the LORD my God, are the One who goes with me. I know that You will not leave me nor forsake me.

DEUTERONOMY 31:6

I pray that You will not forsake me, for Your great name's sake, because it has pleased You to make me one of Your people.

1 SAMUEL 12:22

10

DISCOURAGED

Perfect God, in Jesus' name I ask You to remove from me any discouragement that I may be feeling at this time in my life. Teach me what Your Word means when it says to wait on You and to be of good courage. Thank You. Amen.

GOD, IN ACCORDANCE WITH YOUR WORD . . .

I pray that I will wait on You, LORD; that I will be of good courage, and that You shall strengthen my heart.

PSALM 27:14

I pray that I shall obtain joy and gladness and that sorrow and sighing shall flee away.

ISAIAH 51:11

I pray that I will not cast away my confidence, which has great reward. For I have need of endurance, so that after I have done Your will, God, I may receive the promise.

HEBREWS 10:35–36

I pray that I am confident of this very thing, that You, God, who have begun a good work in me will complete it until the day of Jesus Christ.

PHILIPPIANS 1:6

I pray that I do not grow weary while doing good, for in due season I shall reap if I do not lose heart.

GALATIANS 6:9

I pray that I will greatly rejoice, though now for a little while, if need be, I may be grieved by various trials. I pray that the genuineness of my faith, being much more precious than gold that perishes, though it is tested by fire, may be found

to praise, honor, and glory at the revelation of
Jesus Christ, whom having not seen, I love.
Though now I do not see Him, yet believing, I
rejoice with joy inexpressible and full of glory,
receiving the end of my faith—the salvation of
my soul.

1 PETER 1:6–9

I pray that I will be anxious for nothing, but in
everything by prayer and supplication, with
thanksgiving, my request will be made known to
You, God; and Your peace, which surpasses all
understanding, will guard my heart and mind
through Christ Jesus.

PHILIPPIANS 4:6–7

I pray, God, that though I walk in the midst of
trouble, You will revive me. You will stretch out
Your hand against the wrath of my enemies, and
Your right hand will save me.

PSALM 138:7

I pray that I will not let my heart be troubled.
That because I believe in You, God, and also in
Jesus.

JOHN 14:1

I pray that I will always understand and believe
Your promise, Jesus, that Your peace You left
with me and that Your peace You gave to me;
and that not as the world gives did You give it to
me. Let not my heart be troubled, neither let it
be afraid.

JOHN 14:27

I pray that while I am hard-pressed on every side,
I am not crushed; I am perplexed, but not in
despair; persecuted, but not forsaken; struck
down, but not destroyed—always carrying about
in my body the dying of the Lord Jesus, that the
life of Jesus also may be manifested in my body.

2 CORINTHIANS 4:8–10

11

DISSATISFIED

Lord Jesus, through the power of Your perfect
and error-free Word, I call upon You to replace
any dissatisfaction in my life with joy, hope, and
happiness. Your Word says my soul will be
satisfied and I shall have every good thing.
Through my faith and the authority of Your
Word, I ask that You honor these words from
Your Word. Thank You for hearing my prayers.
Amen.

GOD, IN ACCORDANCE WITH YOUR WORD . . .

I pray that I can do all things through Christ who
strengthens me.

PHILIPPIANS 4:13

I pray that my soul shall be satisfied as with marrow and fatness, and my mouth shall praise You with joyful lips.

PSALM 63:5

~

I pray that I will be satisfied with good by the fruit of my mouth.

PROVERBS 12:14

~

I pray that because I seek You, LORD, I shall not lack any good thing.

PSALM 34:10

~

I pray that I will delight myself in You, LORD, and You shall give me the desires of my heart.

PSALM 37:4

I pray that I will bless You, LORD, with all that is within me, and that I will forget not all Your benefits. I pray that I will not forget who forgives all my iniquities and who heals all my diseases. I pray that I will not forget who redeems my life from destruction and who crowns me with lovingkindness and tender mercies, and who satisfies my mouth with good things, so that my youth is renewed like the eagle's.

PSALM 103:1–5

I pray, God, that You will satisfy my longing soul and fill my hungry soul with goodness.

PSALM 107:9

I pray that I will trust and not be afraid; for You, LORD, are my strength and my song. You have become my salvation.

ISAIAH 12:2

I pray that You, God, who supply seed to the sower and bread for food, will supply and multiply the seed I have sown and will increase the fruit of my righteousness.

2 CORINTHIANS 9:10

12

DISTRESS / SADNESS

God in heaven, You have promised the comfort of the Holy Spirit to me in times such as this. I ask You for a special comforting. Your Word says that while sadness may come upon me, my joy will return in the morning. I pray this, Your Word, for myself. Remove my distress. Take my sadness. Thank You in Jesus' name. Amen.

GOD, IN ACCORDANCE WITH YOUR WORD . . .

I pray that I have done justice and righteousness and that You will not leave me to my oppressors.

PSALM 119:121

I pray that while I may be despised, I do not forget Your precepts.

PSALM 119:141

I pray that while trouble and anguish have overtaken me, Your commandments are my delights. The righteousness of Your testimonies is everlasting. I pray that You will give me understanding, and I shall live.

PSALM 119:143–144

⌒

I pray that in righteousness I shall be established. That I shall be far from oppression, for I shall not fear; and from terror, for it shall not come near me.

ISAIAH 54:14

⌒

I pray that You, God, will strengthen me according to Your word.

PSALM 119:28

⌒

I pray that it will be good for me that I am afflicted, so that I may learn Your statutes.

PSALM 119:71

I pray that You, God, will consider my affliction and deliver me, for I do not forget Your law. I pray that You will plead my cause and redeem me. Revive me according to Your word.

PSALM 119:153–154

I pray that I have great peace because I love Your law, God, and that nothing causes me to stumble.

PSALM 119:165

I pray that if I have gone astray like a lost sheep, that You, God, will seek me, Your servant, for I do not forget Your commandments.

PSALM 119:176

I pray that I will always pray, "Blessed be the Lord, who daily loads me with benefits."

PSALM 68:19

I pray, God, that You will bring me up out of a horrible pit and out of the miry clay. Set my feet upon a rock and establish my steps.

PSALM 40:2

I pray that I will always remember that You, God, are my refuge and strength, a very present help in trouble, and that I will not fear.

PSALM 46:1–2

I pray that since Your name, LORD, is a strong tower, I will run to it and be safe.

PROVERBS 18:10

I pray that I will not let my heart be troubled and that I will always believe in God and in Jesus.

JOHN 14:1

I pray that I will not sorrow, for the joy of the LORD is my strength.

NEHEMIAH 8:10

I pray that I will always live with the realization that my Lord is faithful and will establish me and guard me from the evil one.

2 THESSALONIANS 3:3

13

DON'T UNDERSTAND GOD

Lord God, the words that I am about to pray are Your words. Hear them, please, and honor them. Help me to understand that, because Your thoughts are often higher than my thoughts, I may not always understand Your thoughts and Your ways. Remind me of Your promise that if I will call upon You, You will tell me great and unsearchable things that I do not know. I now pray Your Word to You in Jesus' name. Amen.

GOD, IN ACCORDANCE WITH YOUR WORD . . .

I pray that You, God, will help me to understand that Your thoughts are not my thoughts, nor are my ways Your ways. That I will understand that as the heavens are higher than the earth, so are Your ways higher than my ways, and Your thoughts higher than my thoughts.

ISAIAH 55:8–9

I pray that I will call to You, God, and that You will answer me and show me great and mighty things, which I do not know.

JEREMIAH 33:3

I pray that I will remember that if You, God, are for me, who can be against me?

ROMANS 8:31

I pray that in all these things I am more than a conqueror through Christ who loved me.

ROMANS 8:37

I pray that as for You, God, Your way is perfect. The word of the LORD is proven; because I trust in You, You are a shield to me.

PSALM 18:30

I pray that I will pursue the knowledge of the LORD.

HOSEA 6:3

I pray, God, that You will perfect that which
concerns me and that I will remember that your
mercy, O LORD, endures forever.

PSALM 138:8

I pray that You, God, will make an everlasting
covenant with me, that You will not turn away
from doing me good; but that You will put
Your fear in my heart so that I will not depart
from You.

JEREMIAH 32:40

I pray that I will hold fast the confession of my
hope without wavering, for You, God, are
faithful.

HEBREWS 10:23

I pray that all things will work together for good
to me because I love You, God, and because I
was called according to Your purpose.

ROMANS 8:28

I pray that no temptation has overtaken me
except such as is common to man; but You, God,
are faithful, and will not allow me to be tempted
beyond what I am able, but with the temptation
You will also make the way of escape, that I may
be able to bear it.

1 CORINTHIANS 10:13

I pray that while many are the afflictions, You,
LORD, will deliver me out of them all.

PSALM 34:19

I pray that I will cast my burden on You, LORD,
and You shall sustain me.

PSALM 55:22

I pray that I will fear not, for You, God, are with me. That I will not be dismayed, for You are my God. That You will strengthen me and help me. That You will uphold me with Your righteous right hand.

ISAIAH 41:10

I pray that I do not think it strange concerning the fiery trial which is to try me, as though some strange thing happened to me. But that I will rejoice to the extent that I partake of Christ's sufferings, that when His glory is revealed, I may also be glad with exceeding joy.

1 PETER 4:12–13

14

DOUBTING GOD

Heavenly Father, today I pray the power of Your perfect Word to remove any doubts about You that I might have. The Bible says that Your way is perfect and Your Word is proven. Use Your Holy Spirit to impart Your perfection to me and to remove any doubts that I may have now or at any time in my life. Help me more than ever before to believe and not doubt. And it is in Jesus' name that I pray. Amen.

GOD, IN ACCORDANCE WITH YOUR WORD . . .

I pray that I will remember that You, Lord, are not slack concerning Your promise, as some count slackness, but are longsuffering toward me, not willing that I should perish but that I should come to repentance.

2 PETER 3:9

I pray that because Your way is perfect and Your word is proven, that You, God, are a shield to me.

PSALM 18:30

⌒

I pray, God, that I will always remember that Your hand is not shortened so that it cannot save; nor Your ear heavy, that it cannot hear.

ISAIAH 59:1

⌒

I pray, God, that I am aware that You have said Your counsel shall stand and You will do all Your pleasure. Indeed, You have spoken it and You will also bring it to pass. You have purposed it and You will also do it.

ISAIAH 46:10–11

⌒

I pray that I know that He who calls me is faithful.

1 THESSALONIANS 5:24

I pray that I do not seek what I should eat or what I should drink, nor have an anxious mind. For all these things the nations of the world seek after, and You, my Father, know that I need these things. I pray that I will seek the kingdom of God, and all these things shall be added to me.

LUKE 12:29–31

⁓

I pray that whatever things I ask when I pray, that I believe I will receive them and I will have them.

MARK 11:24

⁓

I pray that I will always remember that You, God, have declared, "So shall My word be that goes forth from My mouth; it shall not return to Me void, but it shall accomplish what I please, and it shall prosper in the thing for which I sent it."

ISAIAH 55:11

I pray that I know that faith comes by hearing, and hearing by the word of God.

ROMANS 10:17

I pray that I do not think it strange concerning the fiery trial which is to try me, as though some strange thing happened to me. But that I rejoice to the extent that I partake of Christ's sufferings, that when His glory is revealed, I may also be glad with exceeding joy.

1 PETER 4:12–13

15

EMOTIONALLY UPSET

Jesus, I am here to pray Your Word and to ask
You to give great peace to me because I love You
so much. As Your Word says, give me a sound
mind and a peace that passes all understanding.
In accordance with Your Word, let me be anxious
for nothing. Thank You, Jesus, for honoring Your
Word in this important time in my life. Amen.

GOD, IN ACCORDANCE WITH YOUR WORD . . .

I pray that I will have great peace because I love
Your law, and that nothing causes me to stumble.

PSALM 119:165

I pray that because I believe in You, God, I will
by no means be put to shame.

1 PETER 2:6

I pray that You, GOD, will help me; therefore I will not be disgraced. Therefore I can set my face like a flint and know that I will not be ashamed.

ISAIAH 50:7

I pray that I will be anxious for nothing, but in everything by prayer and supplication, with thanksgiving, will let my requests be made known to You, God; and Your peace, God, which surpasses all understanding, will guard my heart and mind through Christ Jesus.

PHILIPPIANS 4:6–7

I pray that I will fear not, for You, God, are with me. That I will not be dismayed, for You are my God. I pray that You will strengthen me and help me and that You will uphold me with Your righteous right hand.

ISAIAH 41:10

I pray that I will cast my burden on You, LORD, and You shall sustain me.

PSALM 55:22

I pray that I will always remember that You, God, have not given me a spirit of fear, but of power and of love and of a sound mind.

2 TIMOTHY 1:7

I pray that I will realize that You, God, are not the author of confusion but of peace.

1 CORINTHIANS 14:33

I pray that I know that where envy and self-seeking exist, confusion and every evil thing are there. I pray that I will also know that the wisdom that is from above is first pure, then peaceable, gentle, willing to yield, full of mercy and good fruits, without partiality and without hypocrisy, and that the fruit of righteousness is sown in peace by those who make peace.

JAMES 3:16—18

I pray that while my weeping may endure for a night, my joy comes in the morning.

PSALM 30:5

I pray that when I pass through the waters, You, God, will be with me. And when I pass through the rivers, they shall not overflow me. I pray that when I walk through the fire, I shall not be burned, nor shall the flame scorch me. You are the LORD my God.

ISAIAH 43:2–3

I pray that whatever things are true, whatever things are noble, whatever things are just, whatever things are pure, whatever things are lovely, whatever things are of good report, if there is any virtue and if there is anything praiseworthy—that I will meditate on these things.

PHILIPPIANS 4:8

I pray that You, God, will comfort me in all my tribulation, that I may be able to comfort those who are in any trouble, with the comfort with which I myself am comforted by You.

2 CORINTHIANS 1:4

I pray that You, God, will heal my broken heart and bind up my wounds.

PSALM 147:3

I pray that I am persuaded that neither death nor life, nor angels nor principalities nor powers, nor things present nor things to come, nor height nor depth, nor any other created thing, shall be able to separate me from Your love which is in Christ Jesus my Lord.

ROMANS 8:38–39

16

FAITH

Father God, in the name of Your Son, Jesus, I pray Your perfect Word for myself. Increase my faith. Help me to remember that You said I am to walk by faith and not by sight. Hear and answer Your Word now concerning my faith. Thank You. Amen.

GOD, IN ACCORDANCE WITH YOUR WORD . . .

I pray that You, Lord, will increase my faith.

LUKE 17:5

I pray that my faith comes by hearing, and hearing by the word of God.

ROMANS 10:17

I pray that I will walk by faith and not by sight.

2 CORINTHIANS 5:7

I pray that I will have a pure heart, a good conscience, and sincere faith.

1 TIMOTHY 1:5

I pray that I will always remember that faith is the substance of things hoped for and the evidence of things not seen.

HEBREWS 11:1

I pray that I remember that faith by itself, if it does not have works, is dead.

JAMES 2:17

I pray that I will always have faith and a good conscience.

1 TIMOTHY 1:19

I pray that I will constantly take the shield of faith with which I will be able to quench all the fiery darts of the wicked one.

EPHESIANS 6:16

I pray that I will put on the breastplate of faith and love, and as my helmet the hope of salvation.

1 THESSALONIANS 5:8

I pray that I will fight the good fight of faith, that I will lay hold on eternal life, to which I was also called.

1 TIMOTHY 6:12

I pray that I will draw near with a true heart in full assurance of my faith and that I will have my heart sprinkled from an evil conscience and my body washed with pure water.

HEBREWS 10:22

I pray that I understand that without faith it is impossible to please You, God, and that for me to come to You, I must believe that You are, and that You are a rewarder of those who diligently seek You.

HEBREWS 11:6

I pray that I will be just and shall live by faith.

HABAKKUK 2:4

I pray that I will remember that Abraham believed God, and it was accounted to him for righteousness.

ROMANS 4:3

I pray that having been justified by faith, I will have peace with You, God, through my Lord Jesus Christ.

ROMANS 5:1

I pray that I will count all things as a loss for the excellence of the knowledge of Christ Jesus my Lord, for whom I have suffered the loss of all things, and count them as rubbish, that I may gain Christ and be found in Him, not having my own righteousness, which is from the law, but that which is through faith in Christ, the righteousness which is from God by faith; that I may know Him and the power of His resurrection, and the fellowship of His sufferings, being conformed to His death.

PHILIPPIANS 3:8–10

I pray that I will be just and will live by faith.

HEBREWS 10:38

I pray that I shall believe in You, the LORD my God, and that I shall be established. I pray also that I will believe Your prophets and I shall prosper.

2 CHRONICLES 20:20

I pray that according to my faith, it will be to me.

MATTHEW 9:29

I pray that I will have faith as a mustard seed and I will say to my mountain, "Move from here to there," and it will move; and nothing will be impossible for me.

MATTHEW 17:20

I pray that I will have faith in You, God.

MARK 11:22

I pray that I remember that if I have the gift of prophecy and understand all mysteries and all knowledge, and though I have all faith so that I can remove mountains, but have not love, I am nothing.

1 CORINTHIANS 13:2

I pray that Your righteousness, through faith in Jesus Christ, be revealed to me because I believe.

ROMANS 3:22

I pray, God, that in Your forbearance You have passed over my sins that were previously committed.

ROMANS 3:25

I pray that I will watch and stand fast in the faith and that I will be brave and strong.

1 CORINTHIANS 16:13

I pray that I will examine myself as to whether I am in the faith and that I will test myself.

2 CORINTHIANS 13:5

I pray that I know that I am not justified by the works of the law but by faith in Jesus Christ.

GALATIANS 2:16

I pray that I have been crucified with Christ.
That it is no longer I who live, but Christ who
lives in me. And that my life which I now live in
the flesh I live by faith in the Son of God, who
loved me and gave Himself for me.

GALATIANS 2:20

I pray that I will always look unto Jesus, the
author and finisher of my faith, who for the joy
that was set before Him endured the cross,
despising the shame, and has sat down at the
right hand of the throne of God.

HEBREWS 12:2

I pray that I know the Holy Scriptures, which are
able to make me wise for salvation through my
faith which is in Christ Jesus.

2 TIMOTHY 3:15

I pray that I will fight the good fight, that I will finish the race, and that I will keep the faith.

2 TIMOTHY 4:7

I pray that the sharing of my faith may become effective by the acknowledgment of every good thing which is in me in Christ Jesus.

PHILEMON 6

I pray that it is by faith that I understand that the worlds were framed by Your word, God, so that the things which are seen were not made of things which are visible.

HEBREWS 11:3

I pray that I understand that as the body without the spirit is dead, so faith without works is dead also.

JAMES 2:26

I pray that I will realize that if I do not believe, I shall not be established.

ISAIAH 7:9

17

Fear

God, I pray Your Word to You now to remove any and all fears that I may be harboring either now or in the future. I ask You to remember that my prayers are actually Your words on the subject of fear. Please honor Your perfect Word and remove any and all fears in me. Thank You, God, for hearing my prayers, in Jesus' name. Amen.

God, in accordance with Your Word . . .

I pray that Your truth shall be my shield and buckler and that I shall not be afraid.

PSALM 91:4—5

∽

I pray that no evil shall befall me.

PSALM 91:10

I pray that I will not be afraid of sudden terror, nor of trouble from the wicked when it comes. I pray that You, LORD, will be my confidence and will keep my foot from being caught.

PROVERBS 3:25—26

I pray that in righteousness I shall be established. I also pray that I shall be far from oppression, for I shall not fear. And from terror, for it shall not come near me.

ISAIAH 54:14

I pray that in You, God, I have put my trust and that I will not be afraid.

PSALM 56:11

I pray that I know that You, God, have not given me a spirit of fear, but of power and of love and of a sound mind.

2 TIMOTHY 1:7

I pray that I did not receive the spirit of bondage again to fear, but that I received the Spirit of adoption by whom I cry out, "Abba, Father."

ROMANS 8:15

I pray that in me there is no fear in love; because perfect love casts out fear.

1 JOHN 4:18

I pray that You, God, will give Your angels charge over me, to keep me in all my ways.

PSALM 91:11

I pray that though I walk through the valley of the shadow of death, I will fear no evil; for You, God, are with me. Your rod and Your staff, they comfort me.

PSALM 23:4

I pray that if You, God, are for me, who can be against me? Shall tribulation, or distress, or persecution, or famine, or nakedness, or peril, or sword separate me from Your love? I pray that in all these things I am more than a conqueror through Christ who loved me. For I am persuaded that neither death nor life, nor angels nor principalities nor powers, nor things present nor things to come, nor height nor depth, nor any other created thing, shall be able to separate me from Your love, God, which is in Christ Jesus my Lord.

ROMANS 8:31, 35, 37–39

I pray that I will be of good courage and that You, God, shall strengthen my heart, for my hope is in the LORD.

PSALM 31:24

I pray that You, LORD, are my helper and that I will not fear.

HEBREWS 13:6

I pray that I receive the peace that You, Jesus,
have left with me, the peace You gave to me. Let
not my heart be troubled, neither let it be afraid.

JOHN 14:27

I pray that You, LORD, are my light and my
salvation. Whom shall I fear? Though an army
may encamp against me, my heart shall not fear.
In this I will be confident.

PSALM 27:1–3

18

FINANCIAL PROBLEMS

Heavenly Father, it is not Your will that I should have to contend unnecessarily with financial problems. Because I believe strongly in Your Word, I present to You as my prayers for myself Your very words on this subject. Please honor Your Word and release me from any and all financial problems in my life. I pray Your words in Jesus' name. Amen.

GOD, IN ACCORDANCE WITH YOUR WORD . . .

I pray that I may prosper in all things and be in health, just as my soul prospers.

3 JOHN 2

I pray that You, LORD, are my shepherd and that I shall not want.

PSALM 23:1

I pray that I will seek You, LORD, and not lack any good thing.

PSALM 34:10

⌒

I pray that all these blessings shall come upon me and overtake me, because I obey the voice of the LORD my God. I shall be blessed in the city, and I shall be blessed in the country. I shall be blessed when I come in, and I shall be blessed when I go out. I pray that You, LORD, will command Your blessing on me in my storehouses and in all to which I set my hand.

DEUTERONOMY 28:2–3, 6, 8

⌒

I pray that I will give, and it will be given to me: good measure, pressed down, shaken together, and running over will be put into my bosom. For with the same measure that I use, it will be measured back to me.

LUKE 6:38

I pray that because freely I have received, freely I will give.

MATTHEW 10:8

I pray that on the first day of the week I will lay something aside, storing up as I may prosper, so that there be no collections when it is time to give.

1 CORINTHIANS 16:2

I pray that I will bring all the tithes into the storehouse, that there may be food in God's house. And that I will try You, God, in this and see if You will not open for me the windows of heaven and pour out for me such blessing that there will not be room enough to receive it.

MALACHI 3:10

I pray that I realize that if I sow sparingly I will also reap sparingly, and if I sow bountifully I will also reap bountifully. I pray that I will give as I purpose in my heart, not grudgingly or of necessity; for You, God, love a cheerful giver. And You are able to make all grace abound toward me, that I, always having all sufficiency in all things, may have an abundance for every good work.

2 CORINTHIANS 9:6–8

I pray that I will remember that everyone who has left houses or brothers or sisters or father or mother or wife or children or lands, for Your name's sake, Lord, shall receive a hundredfold, and inherit eternal life. I pray also that I will remember that many who are first will be last, and the last first.

MATTHEW 19:29–30

I pray that this Book of the Law shall not depart
from my mouth, but I shall meditate in it day and
night, that I may observe to do according to all
that is written in it. For then I will make my way
prosperous, and then I will have good success.

JOSHUA 1:8

I pray, God, that because I am good in Your sight,
You will give wisdom and knowledge and joy to
me. But to the sinner You will give the work of
gathering and collecting, that he may give to me.

ECCLESIASTES 2:26

I pray that I leave an inheritance to my children's
children.

PROVERBS 13:22

I pray that I do not worry, saying, "What shall I eat?" or "What shall I drink?" or "What shall I wear?" For You, my heavenly Father, know that I need all these things. But I pray that I will seek first Your kingdom, God, and Your righteousness, and all these things shall be added to me. I also pray that I do not worry about tomorrow, for tomorrow will worry about its own things.

MATTHEW 6:31–34

I pray that You, God, shall supply all my needs according to Your riches in glory by Christ Jesus.

PHILIPPIANS 4:19

19

FORGIVENESS

Lord God, for reasons known to You, I need Your forgiveness. Because I sense that and know that I have need of Your forgiveness, I come to You today, praying Your very words back to You in order that I might be forgiven. Bless now the very words from Your mouth on my behalf. Thank You, in Jesus' name. Amen.

GOD, IN ACCORDANCE WITH YOUR WORD . . .

I pray that as far as the east is from the west, so far have You, God, removed my transgressions from me.

PSALM 103:12

I pray, God, that You will blot out my transgressions for Your own sake and that You will not remember my sins.

ISAIAH 43:25

I pray that I will return to You, LORD, and that
You will have mercy on me; and to You, my God,
for You will abundantly pardon.

ISAIAH 55:7

I pray that You, God, will cleanse me from all my
iniquity by which I have sinned against You, and
that You will pardon all my iniquities by which I
have sinned and by which I have transgressed
against You.

JEREMIAH 33:8

I pray that my transgressions are forgiven and
my sin is covered.

PSALM 32:1

I pray that whenever I stand praying, if I have
anything against anyone that I will forgive him,
so that You, my Father in heaven, may also
forgive me of my trespasses.

MARK 11:25

I pray that I remember that in You, Jesus, I have
redemption through Your blood, the forgiveness
of my sins, according to the riches of God's
grace which He made to abound toward me in
all wisdom and prudence, having made known to
me the mystery of His will, according to His
good pleasure which He purposed in Himself.

EPHESIANS 1:7–9

I pray that I will bear with others, and forgive
others, if I have a complaint against any others;
even as Christ forgave me, so I also must do.

COLOSSIANS 3:13

I pray that I will walk by faith, not by sight.

2 CORINTHIANS 5:7

I pray that if I confess my sins, that You, God, are
faithful and just to forgive my sins and to cleanse
me from all unrighteousness.

1 JOHN 1:9

I pray that if I sin, I know that I have an
Advocate with the Father, Jesus Christ the
righteous.

1 JOHN 2:1

20

GODLY LIFE

Lord Jesus, my Lord and my Savior, more than anything else I desire that I will live a godly life in Your sight. Your words are my prayers. Please honor them by keeping me in the center of Your will in all that I do. Thank You for all that You do and especially for honoring these my prayers. Amen.

GOD, IN ACCORDANCE WITH YOUR WORD . . .

I pray that if I live, I live to You, Lord; and if I die, I die to You, Lord. Therefore, whether I live or die, I am Yours, Lord.

ROMANS 14:8

I pray that if I believe on You, Jesus, who justify the ungodly, my faith is accounted for righteousness.

ROMANS 4:5

I pray that what the law could not do in that it was weak through the flesh, You, God, did by sending Your own Son in the likeness of sinful flesh, on account of sin: You condemned sin in me, that the righteous requirement of the law might be fulfilled in me. I do not walk according to the flesh but according to the Spirit.

ROMANS 8:3–4

I pray that I do not present my members as instruments of unrighteousness to sin, but present myself to You, God, as being alive from the dead, and my members as instruments of righteousness to You. For sin shall not have dominion over me, for I am not under law but under grace.

ROMANS 6:13–14

I pray that I will present my body as a living sacrifice, holy, and acceptable to You, God.

ROMANS 12:1

I pray that I will not be conformed to this world,
but that I will be transformed by the renewing of
my mind, that I may prove what is Your good
and acceptable and perfect will.

ROMANS 12:2

I pray that I will not think of myself more highly
than I ought to think, but to think soberly, as
You, God, have dealt to me a measure of faith.

ROMANS 12:3

I pray that because I am in You, Christ, I am a
new creation; old things have passed away;
behold, all things have become new.

2 CORINTHIANS 5:17

I pray that I will always remember that, You,
God, made Jesus, who knew no sin, to be sin for
me, that I might become the righteousness of
You in Him.

2 CORINTHIANS 5:21

I pray I will remember that those whom You predestined, You also called; and that those whom You called, You also justified; and whom You justified, You also glorified.

ROMANS 8:30

I pray that I will always know that You, God, are able to make all grace abound toward me, that I, always having all sufficiency in all things, may have an abundance for every good work.

2 CORINTHIANS 9:8

I pray that I will remain in the same calling in which I was called.

1 CORINTHIANS 7:20

I pray that if I glory, I will glory in You, LORD.

1 CORINTHIANS 1:31

I pray that I will not let sin reign in my mortal body, that I should obey it in its lusts.

ROMANS 6:12

I pray that I have been set free from sin and have become a slave of God.

ROMANS 6:22

I pray that I will be renewed in the spirit of my mind and that I will put on my new self which was created according to You, God, in true righteousness and holiness.

EPHESIANS 4:23—24

I pray that I will remember that it is good for me to draw near to You, God; to put my trust in the Lord GOD, that I may declare all Your works.

PSALM 73:28

I pray that I will delight myself in You, LORD, and that You shall give me the desires of my heart.

PSALM 37:4

I pray that You, God, will satisfy my mouth with good things so that my youth is renewed like the eagle's.

PSALM 103:5

I pray that I will walk in the law of the LORD and be blessed.

PSALM 119:1

I pray that my ways are directed to keep Your statutes, God.

PSALM 119:5

I pray that I will cleanse my way by taking heed according to Your word, God.

PSALM 119:9

I pray that with my whole heart I have sought You, God. Let me not wander from Your commandments.

PSALM 119:10

I pray that I have hidden Your word in my heart, God, that I might not sin against You.

PSALM 119:11

I pray that I will delight myself in Your statutes, God, and that I will not forget Your word.

PSALM 119:16

I pray that You, God, will open my eyes, that I may see wondrous things from Your law.

PSALM 119:18

I pray, God, that Your testimonies also are my delight and my counselors.

PSALM 119:24

I pray that I have declared my ways and that You, God, have answered me and that You will teach me Your statutes.

PSALM 119:26

I pray that You, God, will make me understand the way of Your precepts; so shall I meditate on Your wondrous works.

PSALM 119:27

I pray that I have chosen the way of truth and that Your judgments I have laid before me. I pray that I will cling to Your testimonies, LORD, and that I will not be put to shame.

PSALM 119:30–31

I pray, God, that You will make me walk in the path of Your commandments and that I will delight in it.

PSALM 119:35

I pray that I will incline my heart to Your testimonies, God, and not to covetousness. I pray that I will turn away my eyes from looking at worthless things and that you will revive me in Your way.

PSALM 119:36–37

I pray that You, God, will remember Your word to me, Your servant, upon which You have caused me to hope.

PSALM 119:49

I pray that You, God, will be merciful to me according to Your word.

PSALM 119:58

I pray, O God, that I have thought about my ways and have turned my feet to Your testimonies. I pray that I have made haste, and did not delay to keep Your commandments.

PSALM 119:59–60

I pray that You, God, will teach me good judgment and knowledge, for I believe Your commandments.

PSALM 119:66

I pray, God, that I will remember that Your hands have made me and fashioned me. Give me understanding, that I may learn Your commandments.

PSALM 119:73

I pray, God, that You will let Your merciful kindness be for my comfort.

PSALM 119:76

I pray, God, that You will let my heart be blameless regarding Your statutes, that I may not be ashamed.

PSALM 119:80

I pray, Lord God, that I will never forget Your precepts, for by them You have given me life.

PSALM 119:93

I pray that Your Word, O God, is a lamp to my feet and a light to my path.

PSALM 119:105

I pray that I shall love You, the LORD my God, with all my heart, with all my soul, with all my mind, and with all my strength and that I shall love my neighbor as myself.

MARK 12:30–31

I pray that You, God, are my hiding place and my shield and that my hope is in Your word.

PSALM 119:114

I pray that You, God, will give me understanding, that I may know Your testimonies.

PSALM 119:125

⌒

I pray that I may gain You, Christ, and be found in You, not having my own righteousness, which is from the law, but that which is through faith in You, the righteousness which is from God by faith; that I may know You and the power of Your resurrection, and the fellowship of Your sufferings, being conformed to Your death.

PHILIPPIANS 3:8–10

⌒

I pray that my steps are directed by Your word, God, and that You let no iniquity have dominion over me.

PSALM 119:133

⌒

I pray that You, Jesus, are always at my right hand, that I may not be shaken.

ACTS 2:25

I pray that I will remember that if I confess my sins, You, God, are faithful and just to forgive my sins and to cleanse me from all unrighteousness.

1 JOHN 1:9

I pray that the work of my righteousness will be peace, and the effect of righteousness, quietness and assurance forever.

ISAIAH 32:17

I pray that blessed am I, because I walk not in the counsel of the ungodly, nor stand in the path of sinners, nor sit in the seat of the scornful. But my delight is in the law of the LORD, and in Your law I meditate day and night. I pray that I shall be like a tree planted by the rivers of water, that brings forth its fruit in its season, whose leaf also shall not wither; and whatever I do shall prosper.

PSALM 1:1–3

I pray that I shall know the truth and the truth shall make me free.

JOHN 8:32

I pray that I will take up Your whole armor, God, that I may be able to withstand in the evil day, and having done all, to stand. I pray that I will gird my waist with truth, having put on the breastplate of righteousness, and will shoe my feet with the preparation of the gospel of peace; and above all, take the shield of faith with which I will be able to quench all the fiery darts of the wicked one. I pray that I will take the helmet of salvation, and the sword of the Spirit, which is the word of God; praying always with all prayer and supplication in the Spirit, being watchful to this end with all perseverance and supplication for all the saints.

EPHESIANS 6:13–18

I pray that I will be diligent to present myself approved to You, God, a worker who does not need to be ashamed, rightly dividing the word of truth.

2 TIMOTHY 2:15

I pray that no one deceives me with empty words.

EPHESIANS 5:6

I pray that I will be a doer of the word and not a hearer only.

JAMES 1:22

I pray that I will not be deceived, for You, God, are not mocked; for whatever I sow, that I will also reap.

GALATIANS 6:7

I pray that I always remember that all Scripture is given by inspiration of You, God, and is profitable for doctrine, for reproof, for correction, for instruction in righteousness, that the man of God may be complete, thoroughly equipped for every good work.

2 TIMOTHY 3:16—17

21

GOD'S LOVE

Lord God, I ask You to love me in a very special way. Help me, Lord, to experience Your love through Your Word and through other ways as well. Thank You, Father, in Jesus' name. Amen.

GOD, IN ACCORDANCE WITH YOUR WORD . . .

I pray that I know that love is not that I loved You, God, but that You loved me and sent Your Son to be the propitiation for my sins.

1 JOHN 4:10

I pray that I love You, God, because You first loved me.

1 JOHN 4:19

I pray that You, Christ, may dwell in my heart
through faith and that I, being rooted and
grounded in love, may be able to comprehend
with all the saints what is the width and length
and depth and height—to know Your love which
passes knowledge; that I may be filled with all
the fullness of God.

EPHESIANS 3:17–19

I pray that I never forget that You, God,
demonstrated Your own love toward me, in that
while I was still a sinner, Christ died for me.

ROMANS 5:8

I pray that I am persuaded that neither death nor
life, nor angels nor principalities nor powers, nor
things present nor things to come, nor height nor
depth, nor any other created thing, shall be able
to separate me from Your love, God, which is in
Christ Jesus my Lord.

ROMANS 8:38–39

I pray that I will remember that You, God, so loved me that You gave Your only begotten Son, that I, who believe in Him, should not perish but have everlasting life.

JOHN 3:16

I pray that I will remember that the person who has Christ's commandments and keeps them is the one who loves Him. And that the person who loves Christ will also be loved by the Father, and they will manifest themselves to that person.

JOHN 14:21

I pray that I know that You, God, have loved me with an everlasting love and with lovingkindness You have drawn me.

JEREMIAH 31:3

I pray that I realize that You, God, will rejoice over me with gladness. That You will quiet me with Your love and You will rejoice over me with singing.

ZEPHANIAH 3:17

22

GOD'S WORD

Heavenly Father, Your Word is such an important part of my life. I pray that Your Word will always be living and sharper than any two-edged sword in my life. I'm praying for Your Word to always be important to me. Thank You, Father, in Jesus' name, for hearing and answering my prayers. Amen.

GOD, IN ACCORDANCE WITH YOUR WORD . . .

I pray, God, that in my life Your word is living and powerful, and sharper than any two-edged sword, piercing even to the division of my soul and spirit, and of my joints and marrow, and that it is a discerner of the thoughts and intents of my heart.

HEBREWS 4:12

I pray that I have been born again, not of corruptible seed but incorruptible, through Your word, God, which lives and abides forever.

1 PETER 1:23

I pray that I never forget that Your word, LORD, endures forever.

1 PETER 1:25

I pray that I put into practice the fact that I shall not live by bread alone, but by every word that proceeds from the mouth of God.

MATTHEW 4:4

I pray that I will always understand and apply the fact that all Scripture is given by Your inspiration, God, and is profitable for doctrine, for reproof, for correction, for instruction in righteousness, that I may be complete, thoroughly equipped for every good work.

2 TIMOTHY 3:16–17

I pray that I know that I have been given
exceedingly great and precious promises, that
through these I may be a partaker of the divine
nature, having escaped the corruption that is in
the world through lust.

2 PETER 1:4

I pray that I always remember that heaven and
earth will pass away, but Jesus' words will by no
means pass away.

MATTHEW 24:35

I pray that I understand the significance of the
fact that until heaven and earth pass away, one jot
or one tittle will by no means pass from the law
till all is fulfilled.

MATTHEW 5:18

I pray that I take to heart the fact that heaven
and earth will pass away, but Your words, Jesus,
will by no means pass away.

MARK 13:31

I pray that if I will abide in Your word, Jesus, I am indeed Your disciple. And if I do that, I shall know the truth, and the truth shall make me free.

JOHN 8:31–32

I pray that my walk with You, LORD, will be so close that my ears shall hear a word behind me, saying, "This is the way, walk in it."

ISAIAH 30:21

I pray that You, O God, will instruct me and teach me in the way I should go and that You will guide me with Your eye.

PSALM 32:8

I pray that I realize the significance of the fact that You, God, said, "So shall My word be that goes forth from My mouth; it shall not return to Me void."

ISAIAH 55:11

I pray that I will not be like the horse or like the mule, which have no understanding and which must be harnessed with bit and bridle, else they will not come near You.

PSALM 32:9

I pray, O God, that I will take Your testimonies as my heritage forever, for they are the rejoicing of my heart.

PSALM 119:111

I pray that I am Your servant, O God, and that You will give me understanding, that I may know Your testimonies.

PSALM 119:125

I pray that I will give attention to Your words,
O God, that I will incline my ear to Your sayings.
Do not let them depart from my eyes and keep
them in the midst of my heart, for they are life
to me when I find them, and health to my flesh.

PROVERBS 4:20–22

I pray, God, that I will know that every word of
Yours is pure and that You are a shield to those
who put their trust in You. I pray that I will not
add to Your words, lest You rebuke me, and I be
found a liar.

PROVERBS 30:5–6

I pray, God, that I will not let Your Book of the
Law depart from my mouth, but I shall meditate
in it day and night, that I may observe to do
according to all that is written in it. For then I
will make my way prosperous, and then I will
have good success.

JOSHUA 1:8

23

GRIEF / HURTING

God, You know the hurt in my life. And You already know other hurts that are yet to come to me. By and through Your Word, I pray that You will console me in a very special way. Wipe away my tears and bring joy back into my life. I pray Your own words for those results. Please hear and honor them in Jesus' name. Amen.

GOD, IN ACCORDANCE WITH YOUR WORD . . .

I pray that You, God, will console me because I mourn, and that You will give me beauty for ashes, the oil of joy for mourning, the garment of praise for the spirit of heaviness so that I may be called a tree of righteousness.

ISAIAH 61:3

I pray, O God, that You will comfort me in all my tribulations, that I may be able to comfort those who are in any trouble, with the comfort with which I am comforted by You.

2 CORINTHIANS 1:4

I pray that I am blessed when I mourn, for I shall be comforted.

MATTHEW 5:4

I pray that I will not be ignorant concerning those who have fallen asleep, lest I sorrow as others who have no hope.

1 THESSALONIANS 4:13

I pray, O God, that You have comforted me and will have mercy on my affliction.

ISAIAH 49:13

I pray that when I pass through the waters, You, God, will be with me, and through the rivers, they shall not overflow me. When I walk through the fire, I shall not be burned, nor shall the flame scorch me.

ISAIAH 43:2

I pray that the Lord Jesus Christ Himself, and our God and Father, who has loved me and given me everlasting consolation and good hope by grace, will comfort my heart and establish me in every good word and work.

2 THESSALONIANS 2:16–17

I pray that I always remember that in You, Jesus, I do not have a High Priest who cannot sympathize with my weaknesses, but that I have a High Priest who was in all points tempted as I am, yet without sin. Let me therefore come boldly to the throne of grace, that I may obtain mercy and find grace to help in time of need.

HEBREWS 4:15–16

I pray that though I may walk through the valley
of the shadow of death, I will fear no evil; for
You are with me; Your rod and Your staff, they
comfort me.

PSALM 23:4

I pray that in this crucial time in my life I can say,
"O Death, where is your sting? O Hades, where
is your victory?"

1 CORINTHIANS 15:55

I pray that Your word is my comfort in my
affliction, for Your word, God, has given me life.

PSALM 119:50

I pray that I will cast all my cares upon You,
O God, for You care for me.

1 PETER 5:7

I pray that You, God, will wipe away every tear from my eyes and that there shall be no more death, nor sorrow, nor crying. I pray that there shall be no more pain, for the former things have passed away.

REVELATION 21:4

I pray that I will fear not, for You, God, are with me. I pray that I will not be dismayed, for You are my God. I pray that You will strengthen me and help me and that You will uphold me with Your righteous right hand.

ISAIAH 41:10

I pray that I shall obtain joy and gladness and that sorrow and sighing shall flee away.

ISAIAH 51:11

I pray that I will walk by faith, not by sight, and that I am confident, yes, well pleased rather to be absent from the body and to be present with You, Lord.

2 CORINTHIANS 5:7–8

24

INHERITANCE

Lord God, in Your Son's name and through Your perfect Word, I pray that I will be fully aware of and never forget the magnitude of the inheritance that awaits me. Give me a vision of that inheritance even now as I pray Your words for my life. Thank You, God, in Jesus' name. Amen.

GOD, IN ACCORDANCE WITH YOUR WORD . . .

I pray that whatever I do, I will do it heartily, as to You, Lord, and not to men, knowing that from You I will receive the reward of the inheritance; for I serve the Lord Christ.

COLOSSIANS 3:23–24

I pray that I will remember that I have been
given exceedingly great and precious promises,
that through these I may be a partaker of the
divine nature, having escaped the corruption that
is in the world through lust.

2 PETER 1:4

I pray that I have an inheritance incorruptible
and undefiled and that does not fade away,
reserved in heaven for me.

1 PETER 1:4

I pray that I will commend myself to You, God,
and to the word of Your grace, which is able to
build me up and give me an inheritance among
all those who are sanctified.

ACTS 20:32

I pray, God, that the Spirit Himself bears witness with my spirit that I am a child of Yours, and if a child, then an heir—an heir of Yours and a joint heir with Christ, if indeed I suffer with Him, that I may also be glorified together with Him.

ROMANS 8:16–17

I pray that I in You, Jesus, also have obtained an inheritance, being predestined according to the purpose of Him who works all things according to the counsel of His will, that I who first trusted in You should be to the praise of His glory. In You, Jesus, I also trusted, after I heard the word of truth, the gospel of my salvation; in whom also, having believed, I was sealed with the Holy Spirit of promise, who is the guarantee of my inheritance until the redemption of the purchased possession, to the praise of His glory.

EPHESIANS 1:11–14

I pray, Lord, that I am aware that eye has not
seen, nor ear heard, nor has entered into my
heart the things which God has prepared for
those who love Him.

1 CORINTHIANS 2:9

I pray that I always remember that in Your
house, God, are many mansions and if it were
not so, Jesus would have told me. Help me to
remember that Jesus has gone to prepare a place
for me, and if He goes and prepares a place for
me, that He will come again and receive me to
Himself, that where He is, there I may be also.

JOHN 14:2–3

25

LONELY

Jesus, I pray to You concerning any feeling of loneliness that I may be experiencing now or may experience in the future. As I pray Your words, help me to remember that You said You would be with me always and that You are my constant companion. In Your name I pray. Amen.

GOD, IN ACCORDANCE WITH YOUR WORD . . .

I pray that my conduct be without covetousness and that I will be content with such things as I have. For You, God, said, "I will never leave you nor forsake you."

HEBREWS 13:5

I pray that I will fear not, for You, God, are with
me. That I be not dismayed, for You are my God.
I pray that You will strengthen me and that You
will help me and that You will uphold me with
Your righteous right hand.

ISAIAH 41:10

I pray that I remember Jesus' promise to be with
me always, even to the end of the age.

MATTHEW 28:20

I pray that I realize that You, God, count the
number of the stars and call them all by name.
I pray that I remember that great are You, my
Lord, and mighty in power and Your
understanding is infinite.

PSALM 147:4–5

I pray, God, that I am persuaded that neither death nor life, nor angels nor principalities nor powers, nor things present nor things to come, nor height nor depth, nor any other created thing, shall be able to separate me from Your love, God, which is in Christ Jesus my Lord.

ROMANS 8:38–39

I pray, Jesus, that I remember Your promise that You will not leave me an orphan but that You will come to me.

JOHN 14:18

I pray that I will be strong and of good courage and that I do not fear nor am I afraid, for You, the LORD my God, are the One who goes with me. I pray that I remember that You will not leave me nor forsake me.

DEUTERONOMY 31:6

I pray, O God, that You are my refuge and
strength and a very present help in trouble.

PSALM 46:1

I pray that if my father and my mother forsake
me, then You, LORD, will take care of me.

PSALM 27:10

I pray that though the mountains shall depart
and the hills be removed, Your kindness, God,
shall not depart from me, nor shall Your
covenant of peace be removed from me.

ISAIAH 54:10

26

LOVE

God, Your Word tells us that You are love and that we must love others even as You have loved us. This is such an important matter that I want now to pray Your very words on this subject to You on my behalf. Honor Your words, Lord, as my prayers for myself. Thank You for the privilege of praying in Jesus' name. Amen.

GOD, IN ACCORDANCE WITH YOUR WORD . . .

I pray that I will love others, for love is of You, God.

1 JOHN 4:7

I pray that I totally understand that as You, God, loved Jesus, He also loves me and that I am to abide in His love.

JOHN 15:9

I pray that I understand the true meaning of love and that though I speak with the tongues of men and of angels, but have not love, I have become as a sounding brass or a clanging cymbal. And though I have the gift of prophecy, and understand all mysteries and all knowledge, and though I have all faith, so that I could remove mountains, but have not love, I am nothing. And though I bestow all my goods to feed the poor, and though I give my body to be burned, but have not love, it profits me nothing. Love suffers long and is kind; love does not envy; love does not parade itself, is not puffed up; does not behave rudely, does not seek its own, is not provoked, thinks no evil; does not rejoice in iniquity, but rejoices in the truth; bears all things, believes all things, hopes all things, endures all things. Love never fails. But whether there are prophecies, they will fail; whether there are tongues, they will cease; whether there is knowledge, it will vanish away. Help me to abide in faith, hope, love, these three; but the greatest of these is love.

1 CORINTHIANS 13:1–8, 13

I pray that I understand that love is not that I loved You, God, but that You loved me and sent Your Son to be the propitiation for my sins. And help me to know that if You so loved me, I also ought to love others.

1 JOHN 4:10–11

I pray that if I have Jesus' commandments and keep them, it is I who love Him. And I will be loved by You, God, and Jesus will love me and manifest Himself to me.

JOHN 14:21

I pray that You, God, will bring to my mind that it is Jesus' commandment that I love others just as He has loved me.

JOHN 15:12

I pray that I shall love You, the LORD my God, with all my heart, with all my soul, with all my mind, and with all my strength and that I shall love my neighbor as myself.

MARK 12:30–31

I pray that I have known and believed the love that You, God, have for me and that I who love You must love my brother also.

1 JOHN 4:16, 21

I pray, God, that I always remember that You have loved me with an everlasting love and with lovingkindness have drawn me to You.

JEREMIAH 31:3

I pray that I know that You, God, love me, because I have loved Jesus, and believed that He came forth from You.

JOHN 16:27

I pray that I will realize that You, God, demonstrated Your own love toward me, in that while I was still a sinner, Christ died for me.

ROMANS 5:8

I pray that I always am grateful that You, God, so loved me that You gave Your only begotten Son, that I who believe in Him should not perish but have everlasting life.

JOHN 3:16

I pray that I am persuaded that neither death nor life, nor angels nor principalities nor powers, nor things present nor things to come, nor height nor depth, nor any other created thing, shall be able to separate me from Your love, God, which is in Christ Jesus my Lord.

ROMANS 8:38–39

I pray, Jesus, that I will take heed to the new
commandment You gave to me—that I love
others as You have loved me and that by this I
will know that I am Your disciple, if I have love
for others.

JOHN 13:34–35

27

LOVE FOR MY SPOUSE

Lord, I pray these, Your words, for my spouse and myself. Honor my prayers by honoring Your own words. I praise You and pray to You in Jesus' name. Amen.

GOD, IN ACCORDANCE WITH YOUR WORD . . .

I pray that while my spouse and I have not seen You, God, at any time, if we love one another, You abide in us, and Your love has been perfected in us.

1 JOHN 4:12

I pray, Jesus, that my spouse and I will follow Your commandment that we love one another as You have loved us.

JOHN 15:12

I pray that since You, God, so love my spouse
and me, we also ought to love one another.

1 JOHN 4:11

I pray, Lord Jesus, that by this my spouse and I
know love, because You laid down Your life for
us. And we also ought to lay down our lives for
each other.

1 JOHN 3:16

I pray, Lord God, that my spouse and I will love
each other, for love is of You; and everyone who
loves is born of You and knows You. But if we do
not love, we do not know You, for You are love.

1 JOHN 4:7–8

I pray, Jesus, that my spouse and I will follow
Your command that we love each other.

JOHN 15:17

I pray, Lord Jesus, that my spouse and I always remember that when we were still without strength, in due time You died for us.

ROMANS 5:6

I pray that my spouse and I will always understand the significance of the question, "Can two walk together, unless they are agreed?"

AMOS 3:3

28

MARITAL PROBLEMS

Lord God, I pray as my prayers today Your perfect Word. I ask You to honor Your Word in this very sensitive area and to be with me in every way possible. I love You and I love my spouse. Be with me now. I ask You to bless the praying of Your Word at all times. Thank You for hearing my prayers. Amen.

GOD, IN ACCORDANCE WITH YOUR WORD . . .

I pray that as for me and my house, we will serve You, LORD.

JOSHUA 24:15

I pray that we have read that You, the LORD God, said, "It is not good that man should be alone; I will make him a helper comparable to him."

GENESIS 2:18

I pray that I always understand that a man shall leave his father and mother and be joined to his wife, and they shall become one flesh.

GENESIS 2:24

I pray, God, that my spouse and I will let all bitterness, wrath, anger, clamor, and evil speaking be put away from us, with all malice. And that we will be kind to one another, tenderhearted, forgiving one another, just as You, God, in Christ forgave us.

EPHESIANS 4:31—32

I pray that we will behave wisely in a perfect way and that we will walk within our house with a perfect heart.

PSALM 101:2

I pray that my spouse and I will be of one mind, having compassion for one another, that we will be tenderhearted and courteous, not returning evil for evil or reviling for reviling, but on the contrary blessing, knowing that we were called to this, that we may inherit a blessing.

1 PETER 3:8–9

I pray that my spouse and I will trust in You, LORD, with all our hearts and lean not on our own understanding, and that in all our ways we will acknowledge You, O God, and that You shall direct our paths.

PROVERBS 3:5–6

I pray that my spouse and I remember that hatred stirs up strife, but love covers all sins.

PROVERBS 10:12

I pray that since my spouse and I have purified our souls in obeying the truth through the Spirit in sincere love of each other, that we will love one another fervently with a pure heart.

1 PETER 1:22

29

Marriage

Holy Father, You have given us marriage as something sacred. It is important to You, and it is important to us. Hear now Your words as my prayers and honor them according to Your promises. I pray in Jesus' name, and I thank You in His will. Amen.

God, in accordance with Your Word . . .

I pray that my spouse and I will not depart from each other.

1 Corinthians 7:10

I pray that we will love each other and that we will love our children.

Titus 2:4

I pray that as the elect of God, holy and beloved, my spouse and I put on tender mercies, kindness, humility, meekness, and longsuffering. I pray that we will bear with each other, forgiving each other, if we have a complaint against each other, even as Christ forgave us, so we also must do. But above all these things help us to put on love, which is the bond of perfection.

COLOSSIANS 3:12–14

30

NEEDS

Lord, You and You alone know all of my needs.
I desire now to spend time with You, praying
Your Word over my needs. I ask that You meet
my needs as only You can do. In Jesus' name.
Amen.

GOD, IN ACCORDANCE WITH YOUR WORD . . .

I pray that I will delight myself also in You,
LORD, and that You will give me the desires of
my heart.

PSALM 37:4

I pray that You, God, will open Your hand and
satisfy my desires.

PSALM 145:16

I pray that You, LORD, will guide me continually.

ISAIAH 58:11

⁓

I pray that I will not spend wages for what does not satisfy and that I will listen carefully to You, God, and will let my soul delight itself in abundance.

ISAIAH 55:2

⁓

I pray that whatever things I ask for in prayer, believing, I will receive.

MATTHEW 21:22

⁓

I pray, Jesus, that if I ask anything in Your name, You will do it.

JOHN 14:14

⁓

I pray, Lord Jesus, that if I abide in You and Your words abide in me, I will ask what I desire, and it shall be done for me.

JOHN 15:7

I pray that I will ask in Your name, Jesus, and I will receive, that my joy may be full.

JOHN 16:24

I pray that I shall know the truth and the truth shall make me free.

JOHN 8:32

I pray that You, the God and Father of our Lord Jesus Christ, have blessed me with every spiritual blessing in the heavenly places in Christ.

EPHESIANS 1:3

I pray that I can do all things through Christ who strengthens me.

PHILIPPIANS 4:13

I pray that you, my God, shall supply all my needs according to Your riches in glory by Christ Jesus.

PHILIPPIANS 4:19

I pray that if my heart does not condemn me, I have confidence toward You, God, and whatever I ask I receive from You, because I keep Your commandments and do those things that are pleasing in Your sight.

1 JOHN 3:21–22

31

OBEDIENCE

God, You have said that obedience is more important to You than is sacrifice. Because I believe that You meant what You said, I now pray Your powerful words. God, in Jesus' name, I ask You to help me be obedient to You in every way and in every situation. Having asked You for it in Jesus' name, I believe that it will happen, and I thank You in His name. Amen.

GOD, IN ACCORDANCE WITH YOUR WORD . . .

I pray that I recognize the fact that You, God, have set before me today a blessing and a curse: the blessing, if I obey the commandments of the LORD my God, which You have commanded me today; and the curse, if I do not obey the commandments of the LORD my God, but turn aside from the way which You command me today, to go after other gods I have not known.

DEUTERONOMY 11:26–28

I pray that I never forget that to obey is better than sacrifice.

1 SAMUEL 15:22

I pray that I will heed Your commandments, O God, so that my peace will be like a river and my righteousness like the waves of the sea.

ISAIAH 48:18

I pray, O God, that I will obey Your voice, and You will be my God, and I shall be Your child. And that I will walk in all the ways that You have commanded me, that it may be well with me.

JEREMIAH 7:23

I pray, Lord Jesus, that I love You and keep Your commandments.

JOHN 14:15

I pray, God, that I know that I ought to obey You rather than men.

ACTS 5:29

I pray, Jesus, that I will always keep Your commandments.

1 JOHN 2:3

I pray that I will walk in Your ways, God, to keep Your statutes, and that You will lengthen my days.

1 KINGS 3:14

I pray that You, God, will teach me to do Your will, for You are my God.

PSALM 143:10

I pray that I will learn Your statutes, O God, and be careful to observe them. I pray that I will be careful to do as You, the LORD my God, have commanded me and that I shall not turn aside to the right hand or to the left. I pray that I will walk in all the ways which You have commanded me, that I may live and that it may be well with me, and that You may prolong my days.

DEUTERONOMY 5:1, 32–33

I pray that whatever I do, I do it heartily, as to the Lord and not to men.

COLOSSIANS 3:23

PATIENCE

Lord Jesus, patience is so important but so
elusive. I pray to You now what You have already
declared in Your Word, and I ask You to honor it
in my life. Bless now the praying of Your Word.
Amen.

I pray that whatever things were written before
were written for my learning, that I through the
patience and comfort of the Scriptures might
have hope. Now may You, the God of patience
and comfort, grant me to be like-minded toward
others, according to Christ Jesus.

ROMANS 15:4–5

I pray that I will glory in tribulations, knowing that tribulation produces perseverance; and perseverance, character; and character, hope.

ROMANS 5:3–4

I pray that I will rest in You, LORD, and that I will wait patiently for You. I pray that I do not fret because of him who prospers in his way or because of the man who brings wicked schemes to pass. I pray that I will cease from anger, and forsake wrath and that I do not fret—it only causes harm.

PSALM 37:7–8

I pray that I will wait patiently for You, LORD, and that You will incline Yourself to me and hear my cry.

PSALM 40:1

I pray that I will imitate those who through faith and patience inherit the promises.

HEBREWS 6:12

I pray that I do not cast away my confidence, which has great reward. For I have need of endurance, so that after I have done Your will, God, I may receive the promise.

HEBREWS 10:35—36

I pray that since I am surrounded by so great a cloud of witnesses, let me lay aside every weight, and the sin which so easily ensnares me, and let me run with endurance the race that is set before me.

HEBREWS 12:1

I pray that I will not hasten in my spirit to be angry, for anger rests in the bosom of fools.

ECCLESIASTES 7:9

I pray that the fruit of the Spirit in me is love, joy, peace, longsuffering, kindness, goodness, faithfulness, gentleness, and self-control.

GALATIANS 5:22—23

I pray that I will wait on You, LORD, and that I shall renew my strength. I pray that I shall mount up with wings like eagles and that I shall run and not be weary and walk and not faint.

ISAIAH 40:31

I pray that I will wait on You, LORD, and that I will be of good courage. I also pray that You will strengthen my heart and that I will wait on You.

PSALM 27:14

I pray that I will hope and wait quietly for Your salvation, O LORD.

LAMENTATIONS 3:26

I pray that I will hope for what I do not see and eagerly wait for it with perseverance.

ROMANS 8:25

I pray that I understand that the testing of my faith produces patience and that I should let patience have its perfect work, that I may be perfect and complete, lacking nothing.

JAMES 1:3—4

I pray that I will be patient until Your coming, Lord. I pray that I will see how the farmer waits for the precious fruit of the earth, waiting patiently for it until it receives the early and latter rain and that I also will be patient, for Your coming is at hand.

JAMES 5:7—8

33

PEACE

Heavenly Father, just as Your Word says, I pray perfect peace for myself. There is no process that I know of that is more important to my having peace than to pray Your words. It is Your words that I pray in Jesus' name, and I thank You for hearing and answering these my prayers. Amen.

GOD, IN ACCORDANCE WITH YOUR WORD . . .

I pray, God, that You will keep me in perfect peace, whose mind is stayed on You, because I trust in You.

ISAIAH 26:3

I pray that Your kindness, God, shall not depart from me, nor shall Your covenant of peace be removed from me.

ISAIAH 54:10

I pray that I will lie down in peace, and sleep; for
You alone, O LORD, make me dwell in safety.

PSALM 4:8

I pray, O LORD, that You will give strength to me
and that You will bless me with peace.

PSALM 29:11

I pray that You, Jesus, have left Your peace with
me. I pray that my heart will not be troubled,
neither will I be afraid.

JOHN 14:27

I pray that I, who have been justified by faith,
will have peace with You, God, through my Lord
Jesus Christ.

ROMANS 5:1

I pray that Jesus Himself is my peace.

EPHESIANS 2:14

I pray that I will be anxious for nothing, but in everything by prayer and supplication, with thanksgiving, will let my requests be made known to You, God; and Your peace, which surpasses all understanding, will guard my heart and mind through Christ Jesus.

PHILIPPIANS 4:6–7

I pray, God, that Your peace will rule in my heart.

COLOSSIANS 3:15

34

POWER

Lord God, I am in need of Your power. That power comes only through Your Word, and that is what I pray to You today. Honor the praying of Your Word and bring Your power into my life. It is in the powerful name of Jesus that I offer up Your words to You in prayer. Thank You for hearing and answering each of these prayers. Amen.

GOD, IN ACCORDANCE WITH YOUR WORD . . .

I pray that in all things I am more than a conqueror through Jesus who loved me.

ROMANS 8:37

I pray that I can do all things through Christ who strengthens me.

PHILIPPIANS 4:13

I pray that I will take pleasure in infirmities, in reproaches, in needs, in persecutions, in distresses, for Christ's sake. For when I am weak, then I am strong.

2 CORINTHIANS 12:10

I pray, Jesus, that whatever I ask in Your name, that You will do, that the Father may be glorified in the Son.

JOHN 14:13

I pray that I always remember that You, God, are able to make all grace abound toward me, that I, always having all sufficiency in all things, may have an abundance for every good work.

2 CORINTHIANS 9:8

I pray, Jesus, that I realize that Your grace is sufficient for me, for Your strength is made perfect in weakness.

2 CORINTHIANS 12:9

I pray that I will see the exceeding greatness of
Your power, God, toward me because I believe,
according to the working of Your mighty power.

EPHESIANS 1:19

I pray, O God, that I understand that You are able
to do exceedingly abundantly above all that I ask
or think, according to the power that works in me.

EPHESIANS 3:20

```
35
```

PRAISE

Heavenly Father, we were created to praise You. Through the praying of Your Word, I petition You to put into my heart a consistent desire to praise You at all times. These words of Yours are my prayers in Jesus' name. Amen.

GOD, IN ACCORDANCE WITH YOUR WORD . . .

I pray, LORD God, that I will sing praises to You and that I will declare Your deeds among the people.

PSALM 9:11

I pray that I will sing to You, LORD, as long as I live.

PSALM 104:33

I pray that every day I will extol You, my God,
and will praise Your name forever and ever.

PSALM 145:1–2

I pray that I will know that great is the LORD, and
greatly to be praised, and that Your greatness is
unsearchable.

PSALM 145:3

I pray that my tongue shall speak of Your
righteousness, LORD, and of Your praise all the
day long.

PSALM 35:28

I pray, O Lord, that You will open my lips, and
my mouth shall show forth Your praise.

PSALM 51:15

I pray, O LORD, that I will praise You.

ISAIAH 12:1

I pray that I will give You thanks, O Lord God Almighty, the One who is and who was and who is to come, because You have taken Your great power and reigned.

REVELATION 11:17

I pray that I will hope continually, O God, and will praise You yet more and more.

PSALM 71:14

I pray, God, that I will enter into Your gates with thanksgiving, and into Your courts with praise.

PSALM 100:4

I pray that You, LORD, are my strength and song, and that You have become my salvation; that You are my God, and that I will praise You.

EXODUS 15:2

I pray that I will proclaim the name of the LORD
and ascribe greatness to You, my God.

DEUTERONOMY 32:3

∿

I pray that I will proclaim, "The LORD lives!
Blessed be my Rock! Let God be exalted, the
Rock of my salvation!"

2 SAMUEL 22:47

∿

I pray that I always remember that You, LORD,
are great and greatly to be praised.

1 CHRONICLES 16:25

∿

I pray that I will bless You, LORD, at all times and
that Your praise shall continually be in my mouth.

PSALM 34:1

∿

I pray, God, that You have put a new song in my
mouth—praise to my God.

PSALM 40:3

I pray that I realize that great is the LORD, and greatly to be praised.

PSALM 48:1

I pray, "Blessed be the LORD, who daily loads me with benefits."

PSALM 68:19

I pray that I will give thanks to You, LORD, for You are good! For Your mercy endures forever.

PSALM 106:1

I pray that You will let my soul live, O God, and it shall praise You.

PSALM 119:175

I pray that I will praise You, God, for I am fearfully and wonderfully made. Marvelous are Your works, and that my soul knows very well.

PSALM 139:14

I pray that my mouth shall speak the praise of
You, God.

PSALM 145:21

I pray that I will praise You, LORD!

PSALM 146:1

I pray that I will praise You, God, for Your
mighty acts and that I will praise You according
to Your excellent greatness!

PSALM 150:2

I pray that I will continually offer the sacrifice of
praise to You, God, that is, the fruit of my lips,
giving thanks to Your name.

HEBREWS 13:15

36

PROTECTION

Lord God, honor the prayers I lift up to You for my protection. They are Your words straight from Your Bible. Protect me at all times through the praying of Your Word in Jesus' name. Amen.

GOD, IN ACCORDANCE WITH YOUR WORD . . .

I pray that my LORD God, who goes before me, will fight for me.

DEUTERONOMY 1:30

I pray that if I will indeed obey Your voice, God, and do all that You speak, then You will be an enemy to my enemies and an adversary to my adversaries.

EXODUS 23:22

I pray that no weapon formed against me shall prosper, and that every tongue which rises against me in judgment, You, God, shall condemn.

ISAIAH 54:17

I pray that Jesus has given me the authority to trample on serpents and scorpions, and over all the power of the enemy, and nothing shall by any means hurt me.

LUKE 10:19

I pray that since You, Lord, are faithful, You will establish me and guard me from the evil one.

2 THESSALONIANS 3:3

I pray that since God is for me, who can be against me?

ROMANS 8:31

37

REBELLIOUS

Lord God, through the power of Your Word, I pray that no spirit of rebellion will ever enter into me. Through the praying of Your Word, keep me free from any rebellious spirit or attitude. I pray to You and I thank You in Jesus' precious name. Amen.

GOD, IN ACCORDANCE WITH YOUR WORD . . .

I pray that I, by doing good, may put to silence the ignorance of foolish men.

1 PETER 2:15

I pray that if I am willing and obedient, I shall eat the good of the land.

ISAIAH 1:19

I pray that I will gird up the loins of my mind, be sober, and rest my hope fully upon the grace that is to be brought to me at the revelation of Jesus Christ; as an obedient child, not conforming myself to the former lusts, as in my ignorance; but as You, God, who called me are holy, I also am to be holy in all my conduct.

1 PETER 1:13–15

I pray, God, that I know that You resist the proud, but give grace to the humble, and that I will humble myself under Your mighty hand, that You, God, may exalt me in due time.

1 PETER 5:5–6

I pray that I am aware that rebellion is as the sin of witchcraft.

1 SAMUEL 15:23

I pray that I will be like Jesus and humble myself and become obedient.

PHILIPPIANS 2:8

I pray that like You, Jesus, I learn obedience by the things I suffer.

HEBREWS 5:8

I pray that I will obey those who rule over me, and be submissive, for they watch out for my soul, as those who must give account.

HEBREWS 13:17

I pray that I know and understand that no grave trouble will overtake the righteous, but the wicked shall be filled with evil.

PROVERBS 12:21

I pray that I do not let sin reign in my mortal body, that I should obey it in its lusts. I also pray that I do not present myself to sin, but that I present myself to You, God, as being alive from the dead, and my members as instruments of righteousness to God. For sin shall not have dominion over me, for I am not under law but under grace.

ROMANS 6:12–14

I pray that I will submit to You, God. That I will resist the devil and he will flee from me.

JAMES 4:7

I pray that while I was once darkness, now I am light in the Lord, and that I will walk as a child of light.

EPHESIANS 5:8

I pray that I will no longer walk in the futility of my mind.

EPHESIANS 4:17

38

SALVATION

Lord, the most important thing in life is salvation. I pray for my salvation through the power of Your Holy Word. Hear these my prayers for my life. Honor them. And bless me with Your salvation. In Jesus' name I pray. Amen.

GOD, IN ACCORDANCE WITH YOUR WORD . . .

I pray that I know that he who believes in Jesus has everlasting life.

JOHN 6:47

I pray that I remember that Jesus has come to seek and to save that which was lost.

LUKE 19:10

I pray, Lord Jesus, that I will come to understand
what You meant when You said, "Therefore
whoever confesses Me before men, him I will
also confess before My Father who is in heaven."

MATTHEW 10:32

I pray that if I will confess with my mouth the
Lord Jesus and believe in my heart that God has
raised Him from the dead, I will be saved. For
with my heart I believe unto righteousness, and
with my mouth confession is made unto
salvation.

ROMANS 10:9–10

I pray that I remember that You, God, so loved
me that You gave Your only begotten Son, that if
I believe in Him, I should not perish but have
everlasting life.

JOHN 3:16

I pray, God, that I understand that You did not
send Your Son into the world to condemn me,
but that I, through Him, might be saved.

JOHN 3:17

I pray that this will be my testimony: that You,
God, have given me eternal life, and this life is in
Your Son.

1 JOHN 5:11

I pray that by grace I have been saved through
faith, and that not of myself; it is the gift of God,
not of works, lest I should boast.

EPHESIANS 2:8–9

I pray that You, God, have saved me and called
me with a holy calling, not according to my
works, but according to Your own purpose and
grace which was given to me in Christ Jesus
before time began.

2 TIMOTHY 1:9

I pray, God, that it is not by works of righteousness which I have done, but according to Your mercy You saved me, through the washing of regeneration and renewing of the Holy Spirit, whom You poured out on me abundantly through Jesus Christ my Savior.

TITUS 3:5–6

I pray, God, that I remember that Jesus stands at the door and knocks, and if I hear His voice and open the door, He will come in to me and dine with me, and I with Him.

REVELATION 3:20

I pray, God, that I have been born again, not of corruptible seed but incorruptible, through Your word, which lives and abides forever.

1 PETER 1:23

SATAN DEFEATED

Heavenly Father, my enemy is Satan. He wants to destroy me. But God, Your Word is stronger than even Satan, and that is what I pray on my behalf. I pray Your Word so that I will defeat every attack of Satan in my life. God, please honor the praying of Your Word and defeat Satan in my life. Thank You, God, in the powerful name of Jesus. Amen.

GOD, IN ACCORDANCE WITH YOUR WORD . . .

I pray that I will be strong in You, Lord, and in the power of Your might. I pray that I will put on the whole armor of God, that I may be able to stand against the wiles of the devil. For I do not wrestle against flesh and blood, but against principalities, against powers, against the rulers of the darkness of this age, against spiritual hosts of wickedness in the heavenly places. I pray that I

will take up Your whole armor, God, that I may
be able to withstand in the evil day, and having
done all, to stand. I pray that I have girded my
waist with truth, having put on the breastplate of
righteousness, and having shod my feet with the
preparation of the gospel of peace, and above all,
taking the shield of faith with which I will be
able to quench all the fiery darts of the wicked
one. I pray that I also take the helmet of
salvation, and the sword of the Spirit, which is
the word of God; praying always with all prayer
and supplication in the Spirit, being watchful to
this end with all perseverance and supplication
for all the saints.

EPHESIANS 6:10–18

I pray that You, God, will open my eyes, in order
to turn them from darkness to light, and from
the power of Satan to You, that I may receive
forgiveness of sins and an inheritance among
those who are sanctified by faith in Jesus.

ACTS 26:18

I pray, God, that You preserve my soul and deliver me out of the hand of the wicked.

PSALM 97:10

~

I pray, God, that the Son of God be manifested in my life that He might destroy the works of the devil.

1 JOHN 3:8

~

I pray that I put off, concerning my former conduct, the old self which grows corrupt according to the deceitful lusts, that I be renewed in the spirit of my mind, and that I put on the new self which was created according to You, God, in true righteousness and holiness.

EPHESIANS 4:22–24

I pray, God, that I understand that even the angels who did not keep their proper domain, but left their own abode, You have reserved in everlasting chains under darkness for the judgment of the great day.

JUDE 6

I pray, Jesus, that I know that You have disarmed principalities and powers, and have made a public spectacle of them, triumphing over them in it.

COLOSSIANS 2:15

I pray that I am strong, that the word of God abides in me, and that I have overcome the wicked one.

1 JOHN 2:14

I do not pray, God, that You should take me out of the world, but that You should keep me from the evil one.

JOHN 17:15

I pray that I will not give place to the devil.

EPHESIANS 4:27

⌒

I pray that I will submit to You, God, and that I
will resist the devil and he will flee from me.

JAMES 4:7

⌒

I pray that I will be sober and vigilant, because
my adversary the devil walks about like a roaring
lion, seeking whom he may devour. I pray that I
will resist him, steadfast in the faith, knowing
that the same sufferings are experienced by other
Christians in the world.

1 PETER 5:8–9

⌒

I pray that at this time I will remember that Jesus
went about doing good and healing all who were
oppressed by the devil, for God was with Him.

ACTS 10:38

I pray that You, God, have delivered me from the power of darkness and conveyed me into the kingdom of Jesus, in whom I have redemption through His blood, the forgiveness of sins.

COLOSSIANS 1:13–14

I pray that in all things I am more than a conqueror through Christ who loved me.

ROMANS 8:37

I pray, God, that my accuser, who accuses me before You day and night, has been cast down. I pray that I overcame him by the blood of the Lamb and by the word of my testimony.

REVELATION 12:10–11

I pray that I am persuaded that neither death nor life, nor angels nor principalities nor powers, nor things present nor things to come, nor height nor depth, nor any other created thing, shall be able to separate me from the love of God which is in Christ Jesus my Lord.

ROMANS 8:38–39

I pray that while I am hard-pressed on every side, yet I am not crushed; I am perplexed, but not in despair; persecuted, but not forsaken; struck down, but not destroyed—always carrying about in my body the dying of the Lord Jesus, that the life of Jesus also may be manifested in my body.

2 CORINTHIANS 4:8–10

I pray that though I walk in the flesh, I do not war according to the flesh. For the weapons of my warfare are not carnal but mighty in You, God, for pulling down strongholds, casting down arguments and every high thing that exalts itself against the knowledge of You, bringing every thought into captivity to the obedience of Christ.

2 CORINTHIANS 10:3–5

I pray that I have sense exercised to discern both good and evil.

HEBREWS 5:14

I pray, Lord, that You will guard me from the evil one.

2 THESSALONIANS 3:3

I pray, God, that Your Presence will go with me forever.

EXODUS 33:14

I pray, God, I will be strong and of good courage; that I am not afraid nor dismayed, for You, the LORD my God, are with me wherever I go.

JOSHUA 1:9

⌁

I pray, God, that You will preserve my soul and that You will deliver me out of the hand of the wicked.

PSALM 97:10

⌁

I pray, God, that You are my refuge and that You will thrust out the enemy from before me.

DEUTERONOMY 33:27

⌁

I pray, God, that the angel of the LORD encamps all around me and delivers me.

PSALM 34:7

I pray that Satan will not take advantage of me, for I am not ignorant of his devices.

2 CORINTHIANS 2:11

I pray that I know that I do not live by bread alone, but by every word that proceeds from the mouth of You, God.

MATTHEW 4:4

I pray, Lord, that I will drive Satan away by worshiping the LORD my God, and Him only shall I serve.

MATTHEW 4:10

I pray that I will gird up the loins of my mind and be sober, and rest my hope fully upon the grace that is to be brought to me at the revelation of Jesus Christ; as an obedient child, not conforming myself to the former lusts, as in my ignorance; but as You, God, who called me are holy, may I also be holy in all my conduct.

1 PETER 1:13–15

I pray that I will have the mind of Christ.

1 CORINTHIANS 2:16

40

SECURITY

Lord, real and true security comes only from You. I pray Your words concerning security for myself. Help me to sense the security that only You can give. Lord, I thank You and I pray in Your name. Amen.

GOD, IN ACCORDANCE WITH YOUR WORD . . .

I pray that I am persuaded that neither death nor life, nor angels nor principalities nor powers, nor things present nor things to come, nor height nor depth, nor any other created thing, shall be abie to separate me from the love of God which is in Christ Jesus my Lord.

ROMANS 8:38–39

I pray that in Jesus I also trusted, after I heard the word of truth, the gospel of my salvation; in whom also, having believed, I was sealed with the Holy Spirit of promise.

EPHESIANS 1:13

I pray that surely goodness and mercy shall follow me all the days of my life and that I will dwell in the house of the LORD forever.

PSALM 23:6

I pray that I am one of those who has come to You, Jesus, and who You will by no means cast out.

JOHN 6:37

I pray, Jesus, that I have heard Your voice and that You know me, and that I follow You, and that You will give me eternal life, and I shall never perish.

JOHN 10:27–28

I pray that I do not grieve the Holy Spirit of God, by whom I was sealed for the day of redemption.

EPHESIANS 4:30

I pray that I will be confident that You, God, who have begun a good work in me, will complete it until the day of Jesus Christ.

PHILIPPIANS 1:6

I pray, Lord, that Your faithfulness will establish me and guard me from the evil one.

2 THESSALONIANS 3:3

I pray that I will remember that You, God, are able to keep me from stumbling, and to present me faultless before the presence of Your glory with exceeding joy.

JUDE 24

SERVING GOD

Lord God, in accordance with Your perfect Word, I pray that I will walk after You and that I will serve You. Your Word is clear in saying that I cannot serve two masters. I ask You to honor Your Word in the area of my service to You. Use Your Holy Spirit to guide me and direct me in this area of my life in accordance with Your Word, which I now pray. Thank You in Jesus' name. Amen.

GOD, IN ACCORDANCE WITH YOUR WORD . . .

I pray that I will walk after You, the LORD my God, and fear You, and keep Your commandments and obey Your voice, and that I shall serve You and hold fast to You.

DEUTERONOMY 13:4

I pray, God, that I know that I cannot serve two masters; for either I will hate the one and love the other, or else I will be loyal to the one and despise the other. I cannot serve You and mammon.

MATTHEW 6:24

I pray that I will worship You, the LORD my God, and You only I shall serve.

MATTHEW 4:10

I pray that I will love You, the LORD my God, and walk in all Your ways, keeping Your commandments, and holding fast to You, and will serve You with all my heart and with all my soul.

JOSHUA 22:5

I pray to You, God, that I will present my body a living sacrifice, holy and acceptable to You, which is my reasonable service. I pray also that I will not be conformed to this world, but will be transformed by the renewing of my mind, that I may prove what is that good and acceptable and perfect will of Yours, God.

ROMANS 12:1–2

I pray that I will be kindly affectionate to others with brotherly love, in honor giving preference to others; not lagging in diligence, fervent in spirit, serving You, Lord; rejoicing in hope, patient in tribulation, continuing steadfastly in prayer; distributing to the needs of the saints, given to hospitality.

ROMANS 12:10–13

I pray, O God, that I shall serve You, the LORD my God.

EXODUS 23:25

I pray that I will fear You, the LORD my God, and that I will walk in all Your ways and love You, and serve You, the LORD my God, with all my heart and with all my soul, and that I will keep Your commandments and statutes which You command me today for my good.

DEUTERONOMY 10:12–13

I pray that I do not turn aside from following You, LORD, but serve You with all my heart. I pray that I do not turn aside, for then I would go after empty things which cannot profit or deliver, for they are nothing. For You will not forsake me, for Your great name's sake, because it has pleased You to make me Yours.

1 SAMUEL 12:20–22

I pray that I will know You, God, and serve You
with a loyal heart and with a willing mind; for
You search all hearts and understand all the
intent of the thoughts. If I seek You, You will be
found by me; but if I forsake You, You will cast
me off forever.

1 CHRONICLES 28:9

I pray that I have been delivered from the law,
having died to what I was held by, so that I
should serve in the newness of the Spirit and not
in the oldness of the letter.

ROMANS 7:6

I pray that I will serve You, LORD, with gladness
and come before Your presence with singing. I
pray that I will know that You, LORD, are God
and that it is You who have made me, and not
me myself.

PSALM 100:2–3

42

SICKNESS

Heavenly Father, in accordance with the perfection of Your Word, I pray that You will heal me of my affliction and restore my health. I need Your help and pray Your Word for that important need to be met. It is in the powerful name of Jesus that I pray these prayers to You. Amen.

GOD, IN ACCORDANCE WITH YOUR WORD . . .

I pray that You will heal me, O LORD, and I shall be healed. Save me and I shall be saved.

JEREMIAH 17:14

I pray, God, that You will restore health to me and heal my wounds.

JEREMIAH 30:17

I pray that I will diligently heed Your voice, LORD God, and do what is right in Your sight, and give ear to Your commandments and keep all Your statutes, and that You will put no diseases on me.

EXODUS 15:26

I pray, O God, that I always remember that Jesus was wounded for my transgressions and He was bruised for my iniquities, and by His stripes I am healed.

ISAIAH 53:5

I pray, God, that You heal all my diseases and redeem my life from destruction.

PSALM 103:3–4

I pray, O God, that I remember that Jesus healed every sickness and every disease among the people.

MATTHEW 9:35

I pray that I will believe that Jesus Himself bore my sins in His own body on the tree, and that I, having died to sin, might live for righteousness— and that by His stripes I was healed.

1 PETER 2:24

I pray that I may prosper in all things and be in health, just as my soul prospers.

3 JOHN 2

I pray, Jesus, that power goes out from You and heals me.

LUKE 6:19

I pray, God, that You have sent Your word and healed me and delivered me from destruction.

PSALM 107:20

O God, I am not worthy that You should come under my roof. But only speak a word, and I will be healed.

MATTHEW 8:8

I pray that the prayer of faith will save me from my sickness and that You, Lord, will raise me up. And if I have committed sins, I will be forgiven.

JAMES 5:15

43

SPIRITUAL GROWTH

Lord Jesus, there is no more powerful prayer
that I can pray than to pray the Word of God
directly from the pages of the Bible. That is what
I do now as I pray for my spiritual growth. I pray
that, as Your Word says, I will take heed to
myself and keep myself in accordance with Your
Word. Thank You for honoring Your words that I
pray to You now. Amen.

GOD, IN ACCORDANCE WITH YOUR WORD . . .

I pray that I will beware, lest there be in me an
evil heart of unbelief in departing from the living
God. I pray that I will exhort myself daily, while
it is called "Today," lest I be hardened through
the deceitfulness of sin.

HEBREWS 3:12–13

I pray that I do not forget You, the LORD my
God, by not keeping Your commandments,
Your judgments, and Your statutes which You
command me today. I pray that I shall remember
the LORD my God, for it is You who give me
power to get wealth.

DEUTERONOMY 8:11, 18

I pray that I have not forgotten the name of my
God, or stretched out my hands to a foreign god.
Would You, God, not search this out? For You
know the secrets of the heart.

PSALM 44:20–21

I pray, God, that I will be watchful, and
strengthen the things which remain, that are
ready to die, for I have not found my works
perfect before You.

REVELATION 3:2

I pray that I will take heed to myself, and diligently keep myself, lest I forget the things my eyes have seen, and lest they depart from my heart all the days of my life.

DEUTERONOMY 4:9

I pray, God, that I return to You, and You will return to me.

MALACHI 3:7

I pray that I will look carefully lest I fall short of Your grace, God; and lest any root of bitterness springing up cause trouble, and by this I become defiled.

HEBREWS 12:15

I pray that after I have escaped the pollutions of the world through the knowledge of my Lord and Savior Jesus Christ, that I not become again entangled in them and overcome.

2 PETER 2:20

44

STRENGTH

God, I call upon You now to give me more strength than ever before. I pray Your Word that You will increase my strength according to Your Word, and I ask You to do that even as I pray Your Word as my prayers for strength for myself. In Jesus' precious name I pray. Amen.

GOD, IN ACCORDANCE WITH YOUR WORD . . .

I pray, God, that You will give power to me and that You will increase my strength.

ISAIAH 40:29

I pray that I shall wait on You, LORD, and that I shall renew my strength. I pray that I shall mount up with wings like eagles, that I shall run and not be weary, and that I shall walk and not faint.

ISAIAH 40:31

I pray that I will fear not, for You are with me. I pray that I will be not dismayed, for You are my God. I pray that You will strengthen me and help me and that You will uphold me with Your righteous right hand.

ISAIAH 41:10

I pray that You, LORD, are my light and my salvation. Whom shall I fear?

PSALM 27:1

I pray that You, God, will grant me, according to the riches of Your glory, to be strengthened with might through Your Spirit.

EPHESIANS 3:16

I pray that You, LORD, are my rock and my
fortress and my deliverer; my God, my strength,
in whom I will trust; my shield and the horn of
my salvation, my stronghold. I pray that I will
call upon You, LORD, who are worthy to be
praised; so shall I be saved from my enemies.

PSALM 18:2–3

I pray that I will be strengthened with all might,
according to Your glorious power, God.

COLOSSIANS 1:11

I pray that I can do all things through Christ who
strengthens me.

PHILIPPIANS 4:13

I pray, God, that You will strengthen me
according to Your word.

PSALM 119:28

I pray that I will be strong in You, Lord, and in the power of Your might. I pray that I will put on the whole armor of God, that I may be able to stand against the wiles of the devil. For I do not wrestle against flesh and blood, but against principalities, against powers, against the rulers of the darkness of this age, against spiritual hosts of wickedness in the heavenly places.

EPHESIANS 6:10–12

I pray that I will take up Your whole armor, God, that I may be able to withstand in the evil day, and having done all, to stand. I pray that I will stand therefore, having girded my waist with truth, having put on the breastplate of righteousness, and having shod my feet with the preparation of the gospel of peace; above all, taking the shield of faith with which I will be able to quench all the fiery darts of the wicked one. I pray also that I will take the helmet of salvation, and the sword of the Spirit, which is the word of God, praying always with all prayer and supplication in the Spirit.

EPHESIANS 6:13–18

45

TEMPTED

Jesus, Your Word says that You know how to deliver me out of temptations. I pray right now that You will now and forevermore deliver me from any temptation that I may encounter. I pray Your Word for me in this area, and I trust You to do as Your Word promises. In Your name I pray. Amen.

GOD, IN ACCORDANCE WITH YOUR WORD . . .

I pray that I remember that You, Lord, know how to deliver me out of temptations.

2 PETER 2:9

I pray that sin shall not have dominion over me, for I am not under law but under grace.

ROMANS 6:14

I pray, LORD, that Your word I have hidden in my heart, that I might not sin against You.

PSALM 119:11

I pray, Lord, that I will not say when I am tempted, "I am tempted by God"; for You cannot be tempted by evil, nor do You Yourself tempt anyone. For I am tempted when I am drawn away by my own desires and enticed. Then, when desire has conceived, it gives birth to sin; and sin, when it is full-grown, brings forth death. I pray that I will not be deceived.

JAMES 1:13–16

I pray that I will remember that if I confess my sins, You are faithful and just to forgive me my sins and to cleanse me from all unrighteousness.

1 JOHN 1:9

I pray that if I confess and forsake my sins, I will have mercy.

PROVERBS 28:13

I pray that no temptation has overtaken me except such as is common to man; but You, God, are faithful, and will not allow me to be tempted beyond what I am able, but with the temptation You will also make the way of escape, that I may be able to bear it.

1 CORINTHIANS 10:13

I pray that I will realize that I do not have a High Priest who cannot sympathize with my weaknesses, but was in all points tempted as I was, yet without sin. Let me therefore come boldly to the throne of grace, that I may obtain mercy and find grace to help in time of need.

HEBREWS 4:15–16

I pray, Jesus, that I know that You are able to aid me when I am tempted.

HEBREWS 2:18

I pray that I will be sober and vigilant; because my adversary the devil walks about like a roaring lion, seeking whom he may devour. I pray that I will resist him, steadfast in the faith, knowing that the same sufferings are experienced by my Christian brothers in the world.

1 PETER 5:8–9

I pray that I will be strong in You, Lord, and in Your might. I pray that I will put on Your whole armor, that I may be able to stand against the wiles of the devil. And that above all, I take the shield of faith with which I will be able to quench all the fiery darts of the wicked one.

EPHESIANS 6:10–11, 16

I pray, Lord, that I will count it all joy when I fall into various trials, knowing that the testing of my faith produces patience. I pray that blessed am I when I endure temptation; for when I have been approved, I will receive the crown of life which You have promised to those who love You.

JAMES 1:2–3, 12

I pray, God, that I will resist the devil and that he will flee from me.

JAMES 4:7

I pray, God, that I will remember that He who is in me is greater than he who is in the world.

1 JOHN 4:4

I pray that in this I will greatly rejoice, though now for a little while, if need be, I have been grieved by various trials, that the genuineness of my faith, being much more precious than gold that perishes, though it is tested by fire, may be found to praise, honor, and glory at the revelation of Jesus Christ.

1 PETER 1:6–7

I pray that I will always know that You, God, are able to keep me from stumbling, and to present me faultless before the presence of Your glory with exceeding joy.

JUDE 24

46

TROUBLES

Lord, Your Word says that You will allow no more troubles than I can bear. Today, even now, I pray Your Word to overcome any troubles I may have. Please honor Your words in my prayers and take care of and strengthen me. It is in the authority of the name of Jesus that I pray. Amen.

GOD, IN ACCORDANCE WITH YOUR WORD . . .

I pray that I shall obtain joy and gladness and that sorrow and sighing shall flee away.

ISAIAH 51:11

I pray that I will be anxious for nothing, but in everything by prayer and supplication, with thanksgiving, will let my requests be made known to You, God; and Your peace, which surpasses all understanding, will guard my heart and mind through Christ Jesus.

PHILIPPIANS 4:6—7

I pray, God, that You will comfort me in all my tribulation, that I may be able to comfort those who are in any trouble, with the comfort with which I myself am comforted by You.

2 CORINTHIANS 1:4

I pray, God, that I do not worry about tomorrow, for tomorrow will worry about its own things.

MATTHEW 6:34

I pray that I will remember that all things work together for good to me because I love You, God, and because I am called according to Your purpose.

ROMANS 8:28

I pray that I will be glad and rejoice in Your mercy, God, for You have considered my trouble. You have known my soul in adversities, and have not shut me up into the hand of the enemy; You have set my feet in a wide place.

PSALM 31:7–8

I pray that my help comes from You, LORD, who made heaven and earth.

PSALM 121:2

I pray that I will come boldly to the throne of grace, that I may obtain mercy and find grace to help me in time of need.

HEBREWS 4:16

I pray, God, that I will cast all my cares upon
You, for You care for me.

1 PETER 5:7

~

I pray that I will remember that though I am
hard-pressed on every side, I am not crushed; I
am perplexed, but not in despair; persecuted, but
not forsaken; struck down, but not destroyed.

2 CORINTHIANS 4:8—9

~

I pray that I recall that though I walk in the midst
of trouble, You, God, will revive me. You will
stretch out Your hand against the wrath of my
enemies, and Your right hand will save me.

PSALM 138:7

~

I pray that I will not let my heart be troubled. I
pray that I believe in You, God, and also in Jesus.

JOHN 14:1

I pray, God, that when I pass through the waters, You will be with me. And when I pass through the rivers, they shall not overflow me. When I walk through the fire, I shall not be burned, nor shall the flame scorch me. For You are the LORD my God.

ISAIAH 43:2–3

I pray, O God, that I will always remember that You are good, a stronghold in my day of trouble; and that You know that I trust in You.

NAHUM 1:7

47

Waiting on God

Heavenly Father, I really do believe that the most important thing that I can do is to pray Your words and thoughts over myself. My prayers today will be Your words from Your Word. Hear my prayers, and help me to wait on You. I pray everything in Jesus' wonderful name. Amen.

GOD, IN ACCORDANCE WITH YOUR WORD . . .

I pray, God, that I will say in that day: "Behold, this is my God; I have waited for Him, and He will save me. This is the LORD; I have waited for Him. I will be glad and rejoice in His salvation."

ISAIAH 25:9

I pray that I wait for You, LORD, that my soul waits, and in Your word I do hope.

PSALM 130:5

I pray that I have become a partaker of Christ if I hold the beginning of my confidence steadfast to the end.

HEBREWS 3:14

I pray that I will wait on You, LORD, and that I will be of good courage. I pray also that You will strengthen my heart.

PSALM 27:14

I pray, God, that my soul waits silently for You alone and that my expectation is from You.

PSALM 62:5

I pray, O God, that I will hold fast the confession of my hope without wavering, for You who promised are faithful.

HEBREWS 10:23

I pray that I shall wait on You, LORD, and that I shall renew my strength. I pray also that I shall mount up with wings like eagles and that I shall run and not be weary and walk and not faint.

ISAIAH 40:31

I pray that my soul waits for You, LORD, that You are my help and my shield.

PSALM 33:20

48

WORRIED

Most precious God, I pray Your very words over my worries. You have promised not to let my heart be troubled if I will cast my cares on You. Based on Your words, I pray that all worry will flee from me and that my joy will return to me. All of my prayers I pray in Jesus' name. Amen.

GOD, IN ACCORDANCE WITH YOUR WORD . . .

I pray, God, that I will not let my heart be troubled.

JOHN 14:1

I pray that I will cast all my cares upon You, God, for You care for me.

1 PETER 5:7

I pray that I will lie down in peace, and sleep; for You alone, O LORD, make me dwell in safety.

PSALM 4:8

I pray that You, God, will keep me in perfect peace, whose mind is stayed on You, because I trust in You.

ISAIAH 26:3

I pray, God, that I will let Your peace rule in my heart.

COLOSSIANS 3:15

I pray that I will be anxious for nothing, but in everything by prayer and supplication, with thanksgiving, will let my requests be made known to You, God, and Your peace, which surpasses all understanding, will guard my heart and mind through Christ Jesus.

PHILIPPIANS 4:6–7

I pray, God, that You shall supply all my needs according to Your riches in glory by Christ Jesus.

PHILIPPIANS 4:19

I pray that I will not worry about my life, what I will eat or what I will drink; nor about my body, what I will put on. I pray that I will seek first Your kingdom, God, and Your righteousness, and all these things shall be added to me.

MATTHEW 6:25, 33

I pray, Lord, that when I lie down, I will not be afraid. I pray that I will lie down and my sleep will be sweet.

PROVERBS 3:24

I pray that I will say of You, LORD, "He is my refuge and my fortress; my God, in Him I will trust."

PSALM 91:2

I pray, O God, that great peace have I who love
Your law, and that nothing causes me to stumble.

PSALM 119:165

I pray, Jesus, that I will remember that Your
peace You leave with me and that Your peace You
give to me; not as the world gives do You give to
me. Let not my heart be troubled, neither let it
be afraid.

JOHN 14:27

About the Author

Lee Roberts is a Christian layman and an active speaker and seminar leader. His seminars have brought change and spiritual growth in the lives of thousands of individuals across America. He is vice president of a firm in the Atlanta, Georgia, area that serves numerous Fortune 500 companies.